LAMPSHADE

BOOK NUMBER TWO

BY

F. J. CHRISTOPHER, F.R.S.A.
Editor of *Popular Handicrafts* Magazine

CONTENTS

v

PREFACE

ONE of the most interesting handicrafts of recent years is that of making lampshades. Although lampshades have been made as long as lamps have existed, it was not until the immediate post-war period that the craft reached such a high degree of popularity. It has now almost assumed the proportions of a small industry.

Thousands of people are now making lampshades at home for a variety of reasons, which embrace the high cost of shop-bought shades, the urge to do some useful form of handiwork, and the need to supplement slender incomes. Whatever the reason for the present great increase of interest in lampshade making, there is no doubt that it is one of the pleasantest of all home occupations. The materials are not costly, the work is clean, quiet and light, and the finished products amply recompense the worker for the cost of materials and the time expended.

I should like to make it quite clear that *Lampshade Making Book Number Two* is quite complete in itself, and that it does not have to be read and used as a textbook together with my first book *Lampshade Making*, also published by Foyles, although I am quite sure that the beginner and the expert will find much of constructional interest in both books.

F. J. C.

BOURNEMOUTH, 1953.

CHAPTER I

Purpose and function of lampshades — points to consider —
variety and scope — shades for particular purposes — materials
— profitable lampshade making — care in working.

In the first place, it is essential to appreciate the function of the
products before commencing to make lampshades. It would
obviously be as foolish to perch a small candle-shade on a tall
and stately standard as it would be to reverse the process, yet
many lampshade makers—professional and amateur—do just as
foolish things in making their wares.

Not nearly enough time and thought are given to the purpose
of the shade before embarking on the actual making of it. Frames
are covered, often very well, but without any very clear idea as to
where and how that particular shade is to be used. There are
exceptions, of course, but for the most part those who do genu-
inely plan and visualize a shade as part of a whole lampstand,
which is in turn part of a furnished room, are the exceptions
rather than the rule. Yet when the making of lampshades is being
taken up either as a hobby or as a means of combining pleasure
with a profitable spare-time business, it is impossible to over-
stress the importance of looking upon lampshades as important
pieces of furnishings in a home, rather than looking upon them
as oddments thrown in when the main furnishing has been completed. If you have in your mind's eye a view of the complete
room in which it is intended to put the lampshade, you will make
just the shade which will fit and finish that furnishing scheme.

If you are making your lampshades for re-sale, it is an excellent
plan to collect as many coloured pictures of rooms from maga-
zines as you can find. Then, before commencing a shade, select a
picture of a room, and make your shade to fit that room. In
recent years great improvements have been made in lighting, and
now nearly every home has a wide variety of lights for which
lampshades will be required.

The shading of lights is a matter depending a great deal on
personal tastes, but a few general rules can be observed with
advantage. First, avoid materials which will give a cold, harsh
light, and choose instead those that, while in no way impairing
the light, cause a soft diffusion of light. For example, a light

9

glowing softly through parchment or amber "Crinothene" in an entrance hall is a much more pleasing and welcoming sight than a plain white lamp would be.

Shades for dining rooms should be not too dressed up and fussy, but at the same time pleasantly warm-looking. Any of the creamy-coloured parchments, ivory "Crinothene" and pinky peach-coloured materials will look well, no matter whether made in paper, plastics or fabrics.

For use in sitting rooms, where reading, needlework and other activities have to be catered for, it is essential that the lampshade should shade the lamps but not obscure the light. Lampshades for the bedroom can be, and usually are, more decorative. They can be as fancy as you wish. Nowadays there is a wide variety of lamps used in a bedroom—bedside lamps, bedhead lamps, lamps to stand on dressing tables and, of course, the ordinary pendant lamps.

Well designed and made lampshades can add considerable charm to a home, and there is certainly a great satisfaction in being able to turn out a beautiful luxury-type lampshade at an economical price. There are many lovely fabrics to choose from, and a very wide range of plastics and parchment-type papers, while lampshades of basket work, raffia and string are all becoming very popular.

Apart from the great sense of satisfaction obtained by making something beautiful and of practical utility, the lampshade maker will find that there is the basis of a very profitable spare-time business in this craft. The work itself is absorbing, and the materials and equipment on the whole inexpensive. Lampshade making is clean and light to do, and can be carried out at odd intervals, without the necessity of setting up an elaborate workroom. One other advantage is that you can start off on the making of a lampshade right away; there is no great amount of tedious practising to this craft. But care in cutting out materials and neatness in working are the only ways in which you can turn out a perfect lampshade.

CHAPTER II

Making lampshade frames: Types of frames — welded frames — soldered frames — solderless frames — tools and equipment — materials — lampshade frame wire — description and sizes — parts of frames — fittings and attachments — making a soldered frame — parts and sizes — types of joints — shaping the wires — supporting the wires — use of "jigs" — assembly — panelled lampshade — shaped parts — jointing device. Frames without solder — suitable types — wire thicknesses — square-pendant shade — shaping the parts — assembly.

THE instructions given in this chapter are for making lampshade foundation frames. It should first be fully appreciated that complete lampshade frames of all kinds, shapes and sizes for every purpose are quite easily obtainable locally, and from mail-order suppliers who specialize in the sale of handicraft lampshade materials. This chapter, then, is included for those workers who would rather make their own frames, or who wish to make a foundation frame for a lampshade of particular design for a special purpose.

The making of lampshade frames is not too difficult a task for the average home worker to tackle, and a certain amount of equipment, and the use of some tools—other than those used in covering lampshades—is required. The kind of equipment and tools will vary to some extent with the type of frame-making adopted. Frame-making can roughly be divided into three main groups, according to the nature of the jointing of the wires. These groups are:

A. Frames with welded joints.
B. Frames with soldered joints.
C. Other types of joint.

Of these, the first method of making frames with welded joints is usually beyond the scope of the average home-worker. Welded frames are jointed by a process known as "Spot-Welding" (a method of jointing metals by melting and "fusing" the ends of the wire), which requires the use of semi-industrial equipment. This is not described here, as information about the setting up of plant and equipment for spot-welding can be obtained from the manufacturers of such equipment.

Methods B and C are those most suitable for the worker at

home, and these may be simplified in description by describing them as *making frames with solder* and *making frames without solder*. For both kinds of frame-making a pair of really good pliers, such as those illustrated in Fig. 1 (with strong jaws and side cutting edges), will be required. These are used for cutting and bending wires. A smaller pair of pliers may also be required, but these are not essential to commence with.

For soldered frames it will be necessary to use a soldering iron, and an electrically heated iron, such as the type illustrated in Fig. 1, is best if many frames are to be made. When buying an

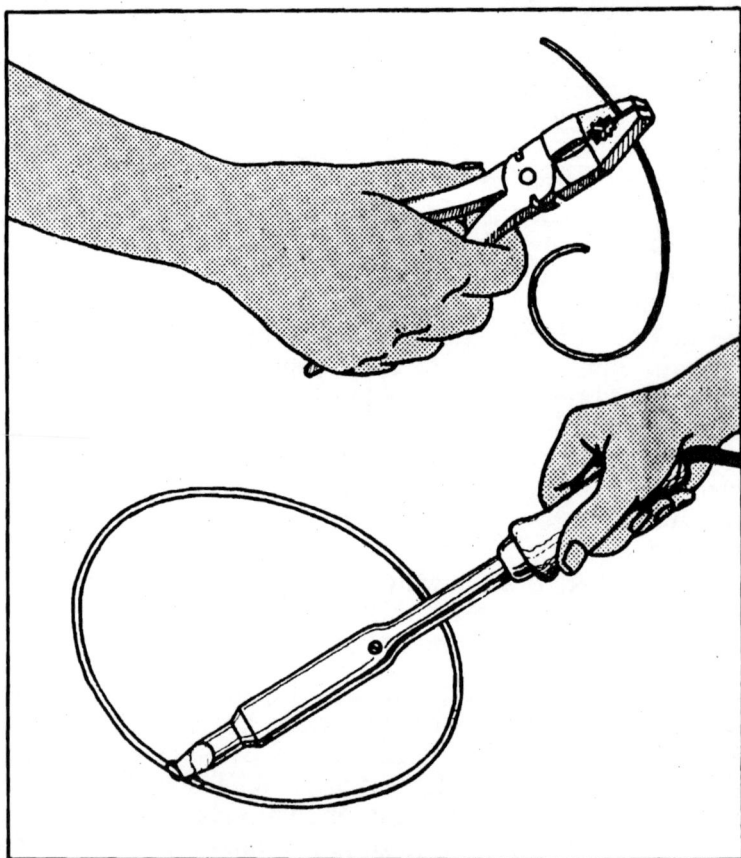

FIG. I. TOOLS IN USE

electric soldering iron, make certain that it is suitable for use with the voltage of the house mains. A 60-watt soldering iron will provide a steady heat to the "bit." The soldering iron should be properly connected to a three-point plug to ensure that it is safely earthed before use.

Solder and flux are required for making soldered frames. These materials may be purchased together in the form of "cored" solder, which is supplied as coils of tube solder, the centre of the tube being filled with flux. The use of solder of this kind enables the worker to make good strong joints in less time than in using solder and flux separately.

The main essential in making lampshade frames is, of course, wire. Not any old wire will do. The most suitable wire is mild-steel tinned wire which can be easily bent to shape and will readily "take" soldering. This wire is usually obtainable locally in coils varying in weight from 1 to 28 lb. When buying wire, make sure it has a bright, shiny surface, or it may be difficult to work and solder. Copper wire is also suitable for lampshade making. All kinds of wire should be stored flat and should be kept away from anything of a corrosive or greasy nature.

The wire used for making a lampshade foundation frame must obviously be suitable in thickness and strength for the particular size and type of lampshade being made. To give a simple example, it would be foolish to use wire light enough for a candle lamp-shade for a large frame for a standard lamp. The following is a guide to suitability of wire gauges for frames for particular purposes (the abbreviation s.w.g. stands for Standard Wire Gauge).

For large frames, suitable for standard-lamp shades, large pendant-lamp shades and large table-lamp shades—in fact, for all large shades—12 s.w.g. should be used.

For frames of medium size, such as those for shades for pendant- and table-lamp use, and for some kinds of bed lamps, 14 s.w.g. should be used.

For making small frames for use on wall lamps, small candle lamps on chandeliers, and most kinds of bed lamps, wire of 16 s.w.g. should be used.

These wire gauges only apply to wire used for making soldered frames. Frames without solder require the use of thinner wire, and this will be fully described later in this chapter.

There are, of course, many kinds of frames for different purposes, and these are shown in some of the illustrations throughout

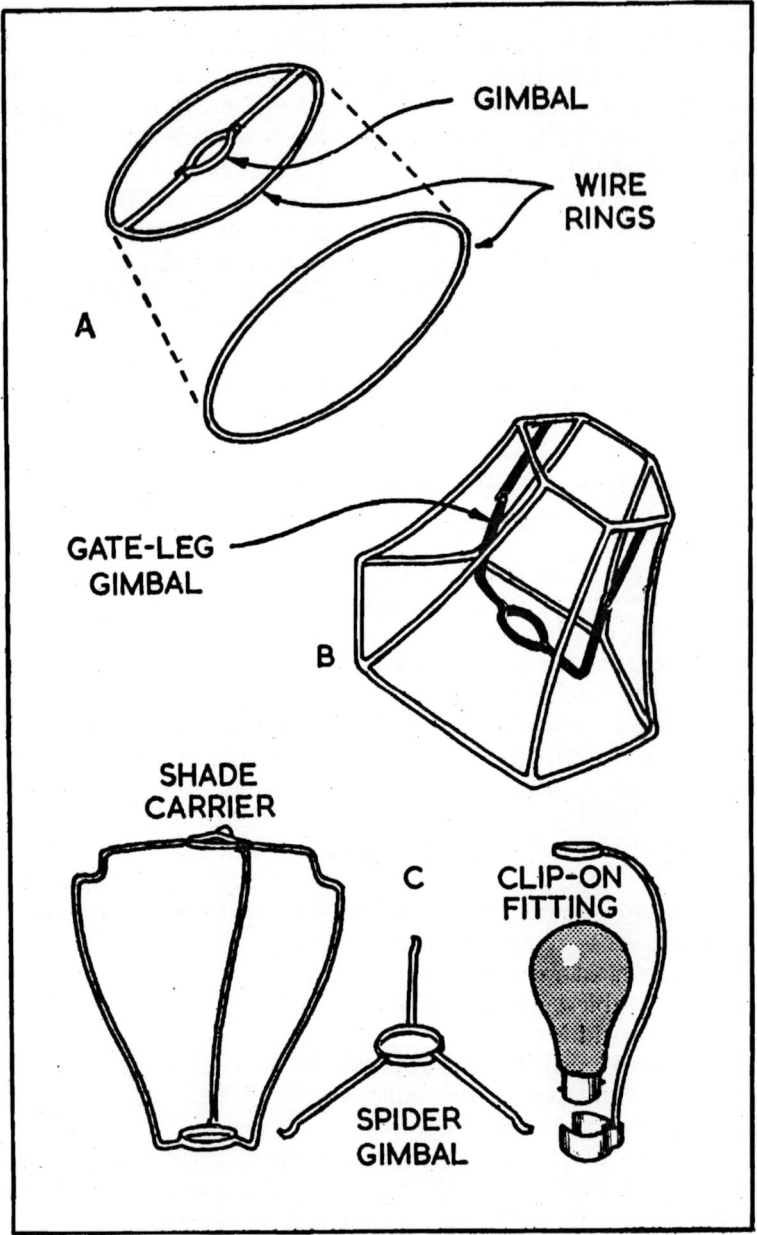

GIMBAL

WIRE RINGS

A

GATE-LEG GIMBAL

B

SHADE CARRIER

C

CLIP-ON FITTING

SPIDER GIMBAL

FIG. 2.   FRAMES AND FITTINGS

this book. Fig. 2 shows some typical frames and illustrates the main features general to all types of frames. Fig. 2a shows an exploded "Empire" frame which has a "top member" in the shape of a ring, a "base member" also circular in shape, and a "gimbal." The gimbal is simply a small wire ring which is attached to the top member by a short piece of wire either side of the top. The gimbal fits over the lamp-holder socket and is held in place on the socket with a screwed retaining ring.

Fig. 2b shows a frame with shaped "side members" which divide the frame into panels. This frame has no top gimbal ring fitted to the top member, but it is shown fitted with a "gate-leg" gimbal. This form of gimbal fitting, which is hinged, allows the frame to be used for a table lamp. Gate-leg gimbals can be purchased ready-made for attachment by soldering to frames made at home.

Fig. 2c shows other types of fittings for use with lampshade frames of different types, including a "spider gimbal," which allows the top member of a frame to rest in grooves at the ends of the arms, a "clip-on" fitment for very small shades, a "shade carrier" for use with large standard lamps. The gimbal attachment can be fitted to a pendant lamp to convert it to use over a table lamp. These are the main fitments. Any others are mentioned in later chapters describing their uses.

To make a soldered lampshade it is necessary to cut wires to length for the various parts of the frame, bend the wires to shape, and solder each joint. Therefore, when cutting wires to length, it will be necessary to allow extra for any overlapping joints. To illustrate the making of a lampshade frame, the construction of an "Empire" shade with side members is described and the parts are illustrated in Fig. 3.

This lampshade has a top diameter of 5 in., the base has a diameter of 8 in., and the sides of the lampshade are also 8 in. Nine pieces of wire are required to make the frame. These pieces are: one for the top, one for the base, four pieces (one for each) for the side members, a piece for the gimbal, and two short pieces for the gimbal supports. The piece of wire for the top should measure 5 in. by $3\frac{1}{7}$ in. plus $\frac{1}{4}$ in., which allows for overlapping the joint. Therefore this piece should be just over 16 in. long. The piece for the circular base should be 8 in. by $3\frac{1}{7}$ in. plus $\frac{1}{4}$ in. (about $25\frac{1}{2}$ in.), which is equal to the circumference plus $\frac{1}{4}$ in. for overlapping. The pieces for the side members should be 8 in. long plus

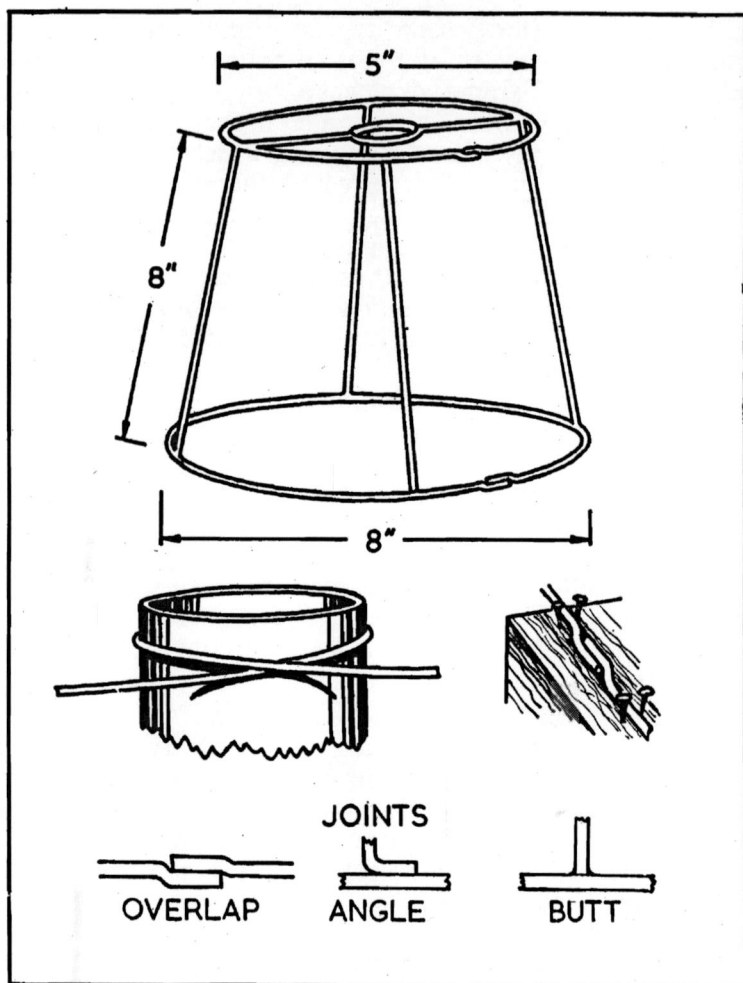

FIG. 3. EXPLODED " EMPIRE "

$\frac{3}{4}$ in., which allows $\frac{3}{8}$ in. at each end of the wire to bend over for jointing. The diameter of the small gimbal ring should be $1\frac{1}{8}$ in., and the supporting pieces which hold the gimbal in place on the top ring should be 2 in. to allow for overlapping joints.

The illustration Fig. 3 shows how all the joints of the lampshade are made. The top ring and the base ring both have overlapping joints, and the wire should be bent to the shape shown in the illustration. The side members can be bent over at right angles at top and bottom to make the joints shown, or they could simply be "butted" on to the wire. The gimbal-ring supporting pieces are attached under the top ring and under the gimbal ring.

To make the frame it will be necessary to shape the top and base, and this can be done by bending the wires round a tin of suitable size (smaller than the size of the finished piece), as shown in the illustration. If this is done successfully, perfect circles should be formed. The next part of the work consists of soldering the joints of the top and base rings, and the appearance of the finished joint where the wires overlap is shown in the illustration.

To hold the wires in place while the ends are being soldered, four nails should be hammered into a piece of wood or bench top as shown. With the ends of the top and base rims firmly and neatly soldered, the side members should be attached. To do this accurately it will be necessary to support the wires by means of wooden shapes. These shapes are shown in Fig. 4, where it will be seen that for the frame described it will be necessary to cut two pieces of wood to shape and fit them together with a simple halved joint. This will suffice to hold the top and bottom rings in position, and the ends of the shaped pieces of wood will form a rest for the side members, which may then be soldered to the main frame. The last piece to make is the gimbal, and the small ring may be shaped by bending the wire over a piece of round wood such as a broom handle. With this done, the ends of the gimbal ring should be soldered and the two supporting wires attached first to the ring, then to the top of the frame.

Once the wooden pattern or "jig" has been made it can be used for making hundreds of lampshades of the same size and shape. For each different shape or size made it will be necessary to construct another simple wood pattern so that the parts may be held in place while the joints are being soldered.

Also shown in Fig. 4 is a wooden jig for a shaped frame, and these two illustrations should be sufficient to give the frame maker the idea of the process of construction. In the case of "Empire" frames without side-members, special jigs can be made for the top and bottom rings. These consist of a circular piece of wood lipped with a piece of three-ply, and if necessary the top of the centre piece can be protected by adding asbestos.

It is quite a simple matter to shape a piece of wire for the round "Empire" frame, but it will be found rather more difficult to

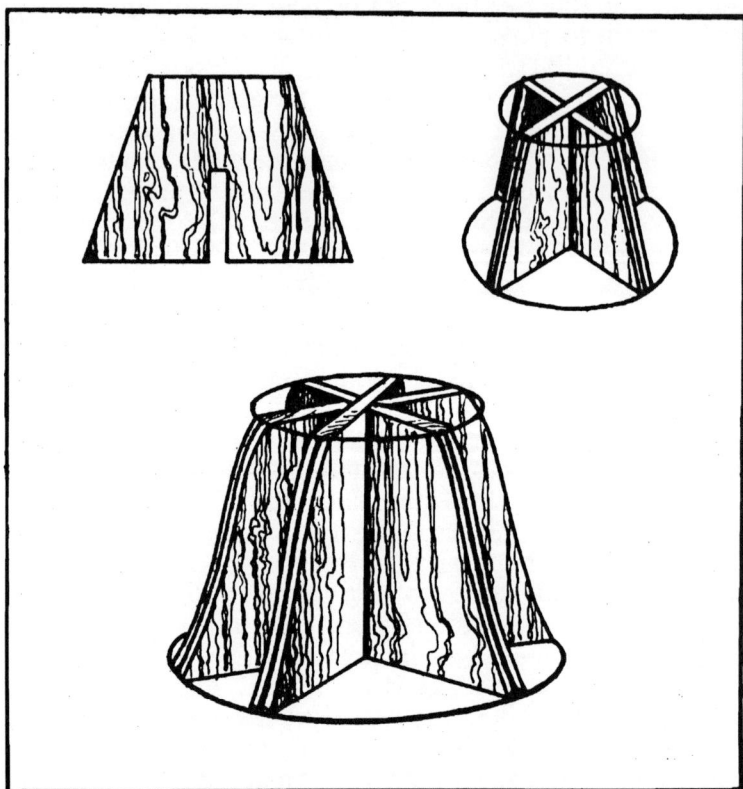

FIG. 4. WOOD SHAPES

shape wires for other types of frame, such as the panel frame
illustrated in Fig. 5, which has a shaped top and base and side
members. To shape the scalloped base it will be necessary to cut
a piece of wood to the shape of a semicircle and attach it to a
bench top. With this done, two nails or screws should be firmly
positioned as shown in the illustration (Fig. 5). The wire for the
base is then cut to length and shaped by inserting one end between
one of the nails and the jig, bending it firmly round the part of the
wood shape, then bending the end of the wire down to form the
end of the scallop. This is repeated to form all the scallops of the
frame to shape.

For the side members it will be necessary to make a two-part

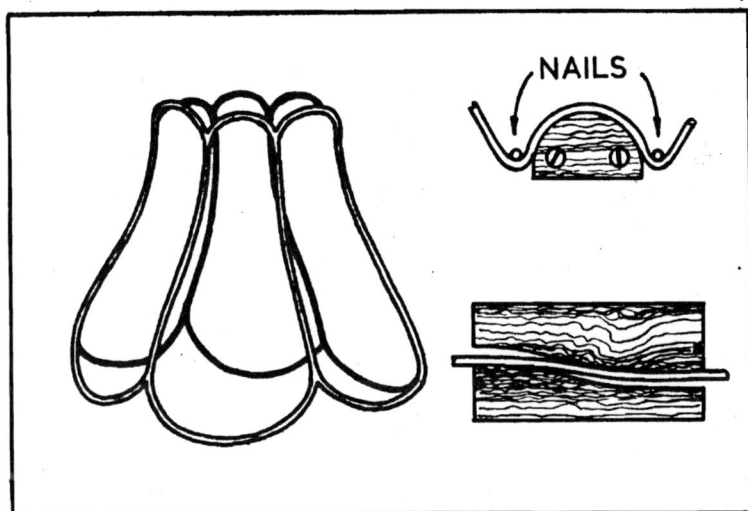

FIG. 5.   PANELLED FRAME

jig. This is illustrated in Fig. 5. It consists simply of two pieces of
wood which are cut to the shape of the side member so that they
fit together snugly. With these made, the wire is then cut to length,
placed between the two pieces of the jig, which are then placed in
a bench vice and forced together. Obviously, a very hard wood
should be used for making parts of the jig, or alternatively the
shaped sides may be protected with a strip of thin metal. Of
course, it will be necessary to make a set of jigs and patterns for
each frame being made, if it is intended to practise this part of the
craft as a commercial venture. If only one or two frames of the
same shape and size are being made, it is not necessary to go to
all the trouble of making jigs. It should be possible for the worker
to shape the parts by hand with a pair of pliers, and in the case
of shaped side members and bases, pattern outlines can be drawn
on a stiff piece of paper and wire bent to these shapes.
     All the parts of panelled lampshades should be firmly soldered
together.
     Another method of jointing wires in lampshade making, if only
a few are being made, can be done by using a simple device known
as the "Wirejoint," and this is illustrated in Fig. 6. By this method,
thin lampshade wires can be joined together in a matter of seconds

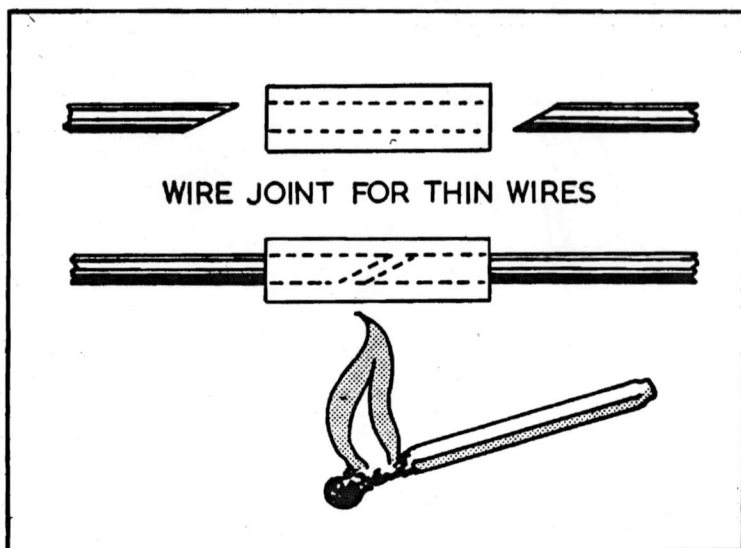

WIRE JOINT FOR THIN WIRES

FIG. 6.   WIRE JOINT

with a perfect soldered joint in one operation, using no other tools than a lighted match. The "Wirejoint" consists of a ceramic insulating tube or connector, which contains a central lining of solder and non-corrosive flux. The ends of the wires should overlap inside the tube. The use of a match completes the joint.

Although to make any quantity of wire lampshade frames requires a soldering iron, the home craftsman who wishes to make just a few frames can quite easily do this by the solderless method here described. This is not suitable for all types of frames, but quite a variety of bed lamps, table lamps and pendant shades can be made by this method.

Fig. 7 shows several suitable styles, and although the instructions given here are for a square pendant, the other types are just as easy to make. For making these frames without solder, you will need a pair of side-cutting pliers, a ruler, a pair of scissors, some insulating tape, some bias tape and, of course, the necessary wire. When purchasing the wire it should be ensured that it is the correct gauge for the type of frame you wish to make. Generally speaking, all small frames, such as those for candle lamps, wall lamps and the small types of bed lamps which are soldered, are made from 16 s.w.g. wire, but for making these without solder, 18 s.w.g. is recommended. Medium-sized frames, such as the larger-type bed lamps, table lamps, pendant lamps and some styles of hanging bowl shades which are soldered, are best made with 14 s.w.g., but for solderless frames you are advised to use 16 s.w.g. However, should you decide on a large frame, either a hanging bowl shape or a standard lampshade which, when soldered, is normally made from 12 s.w.g. wire, for a solderless frame you should use 14 s.w.g. It is important that the correct thickness of wire is used in each case. These are, however, only intended as a guide, and if you are making an in-between-sized frame you must select the most suitable thickness of wire for the particular type and purpose of the shade. Generally speaking, for

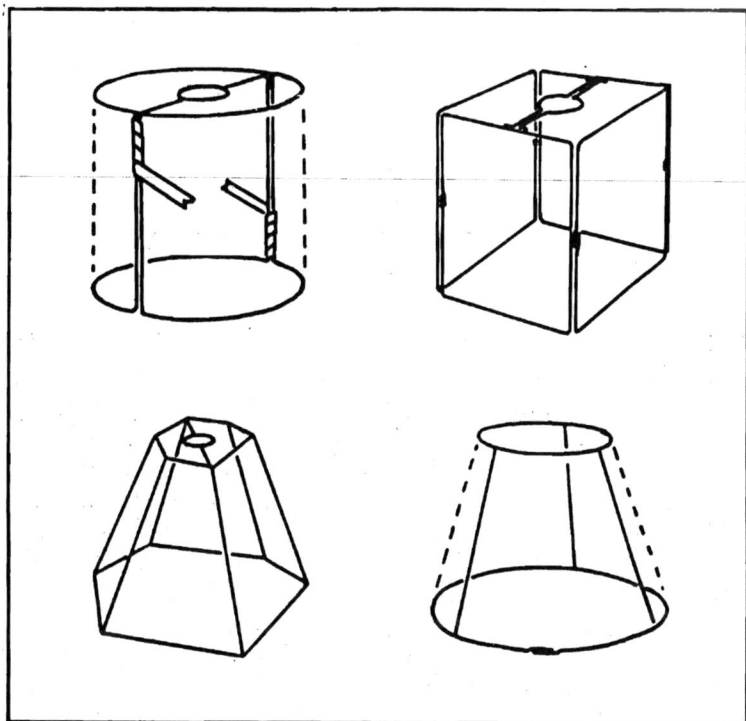

FIG. 7. SOLDERLESS FRAMES

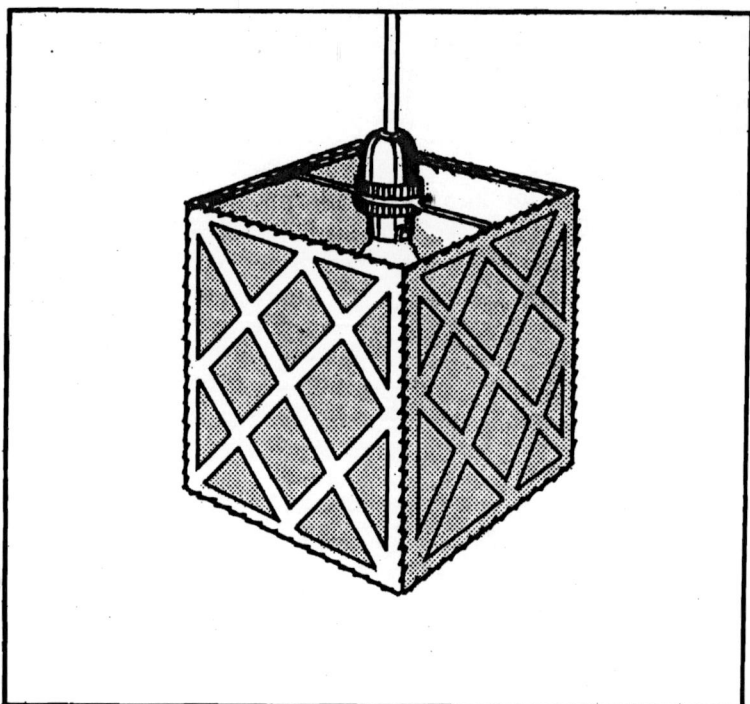

FIG. 8. FRAME WITHOUT SOLDER

solderless frames a thinner wire is used than that used for a soldered frame.

The frame shown in Fig. 8 is a very simple square pendant type. This type of frame is very suitable for use in an entrance hall, and frames of this type may be covered with a great variety of materials. It is a very useful basic shape, and can be made in any size. The frame is made by forming the wire to the shape of each part separately and then binding them together. Exact dimensions are not given, as the lampshade maker will probably wish to make a frame to fit personal requirements.

Commence by making six squares of wire, one for each side (these obviously must match exactly) and the top and base. The corners are bent with the pliers, and it may be necessary to make several adjustments to ensure accurate fitting when assembling. It is best to make thegimbal after the frame has been assembled. This

assures accurate fitting. Now take all the parts and try them against each other to ensure that they will make an accurate whole. The frame is assembled by binding the parts together with adhesive tape.

To assemble, take two squares and bind them together top and bottom with insulating tape, as shown in the illustration Fig. 9. Bind the adhesive tape tightly at the corners and ends of the wires. It is never necessary to bind all the wire, but you must to some extent use your own judgment as to the exact amount of binding required for any one frame. Overlap the tape when binding, as this avoids a lumpy joint, which may show when the shade is covered. Join the other squares to the frame in the same manner. It will be necessary to bind them very carefully to avoid getting the joints large and lumpy. Fig. 9 shows the steps in binding

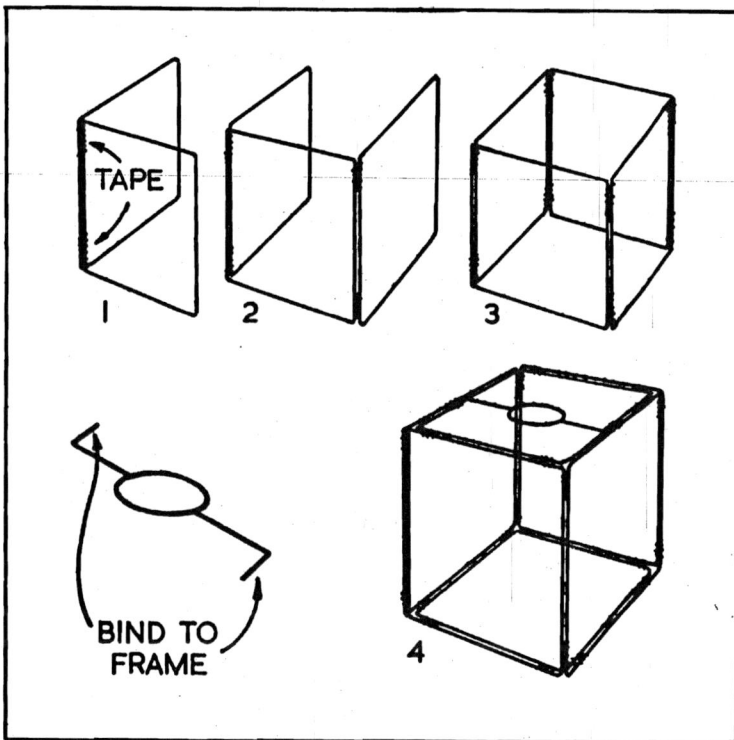

FIG. 9. JOINING THE PARTS

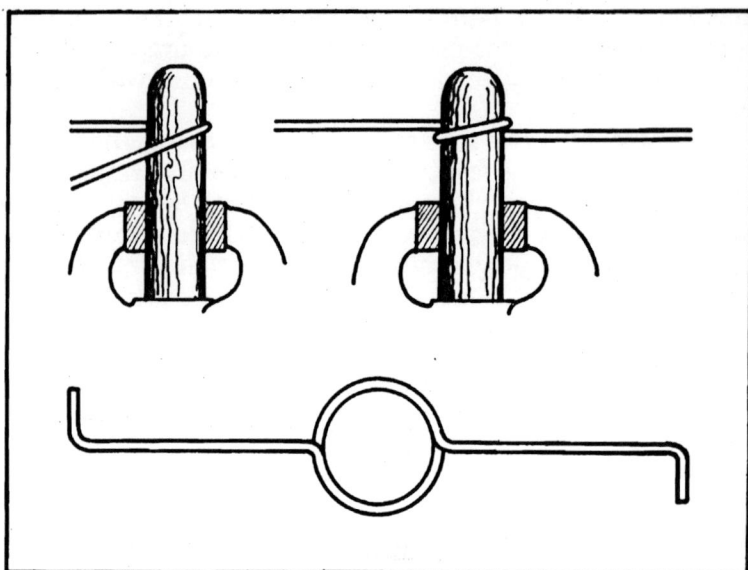

FIG. 10. ONE PIECE GIMBAL

the parts together. Place the gimbal ring in position and bind carefully. The frame is now complete and ready for binding with bias tape before covering, and all the wires should be bound except the gimbal ring, to make the frame firm and rigid.

The gimbal ring and supports can be made in one piece and the ends bent over for attachment to the frame. A method of making one-piece gimbals for this type of frame and others is illustrated in Fig. 10. To make this type of gimbal a piece of round wood should be secured to a flat piece of wood. The round piece should be 1⅛ in. in diameter. The wire—of suitable gauge for the type of frame being made—should be placed against the front of the round piece of wood and the ends bent to form an inverted U. The ends should then be crossed at the front of the shaping piece, then each wire bent with pliers at right angles to the ring.

CHAPTER III

*Covering materials: Choice and individual requirements —
types of material — plastics — "Crinothene" — heat sealing
— "Rilfoil" — description and uses — Cellulose Acetate and
its use in lampshade making. Fabrics for lampshade making —
parchment, vellum and papers — other materials. Braid, gimp
and trimmings.*

THE covering of lampshades for the home is very much a matter
of personal taste and suitability. It is difficult to make hard-and-
fast rules as to which materials are best for lampshade covering.
Some are perhaps more practical in use than others, but even the
value of durability is debatable. After all, it may be that one
prefers a shade which is pretty but will last only a short time and
then have to be re-covered, rather than to have a plainer shade
which will last for years.

Lampshades have been made from practically every material—
string, raffia, cane, "Cellophane," wood, and many others. Roughly speaking, they fall into four groups—plastics, fabrics, papers and
miscellaneous.

Plastics are perhaps the most popular at present, and there is a
huge variety offered by the manufacturers. "Crinothene" is probably the best-known plastic covering, and it certainly has much
to recommend it, because of the ease with which even the most
inexperienced person can work it and its wide colour range of
soft pastel shades which do not colour the light given out by the
lamp. "Crinothene" has very great light-diffusion properties and
is in every way suitable for covering lampshades.

"Crinothene" is a flexible sheet material; it is very tough,
though having a very dainty appearance; it is non-tacky, durable
and light. The surface has an attractive patterned, crêpe-like
appearance, and is produced in many lovely shades—blue, pink,
peach, amber, green, mauve, ivory and natural. It is easily washed
in warm soapy water without fear of damage, distortion or fading.
"Crinothene" does not contain any plasticizer, and under normal
conditions will show no signs of hardening with age or becoming brittle. It is sold by all handicraft dealers by the yard. The
width is normally 34 in., while the thickness of the material
averages about 0 030 in. "Crinothene" may be cut easily with
scissors or knife and can be punched and stapled without any

difficulty. A wax pencil or chalk are the most suitable for tracing patterns on to the material.

"Crinothene" can be stitched with cotton or wire, the most satisfactory joint being obtained by six to eight stitches to the inch. Satisfactory joints can also be made by heat-sealing in the following manner. Fasten your material so that the overlapping edges are held firmly in place. The heat-sealing may be done with a heated tool; an ordinary soldering iron, the type which is heated over a gas ring, may be used, or if you work carefully a clean poker will do the job. However, to obtain the best results an electrically heated soldering iron should be used. Whichever tool you use, obviously it must be clean, and it will be necessary to experiment on a spare piece of "Crinothene."

After heating the tool, turn off the heat and commence working the material. Start at the top of the joint and work down, using a stroking movement with the tool. Do not press the tool into the material. Now work along the joint on the inside. Next, on the right side of the "Crinothene," and using a heated small modelling tool or steel knitting needle, roughen the surface of the joint. Leave the "Crinothene" to cool and harden. The strength of the bond obtained by heat-sealing is the same as that of the "Crinothene" itself.

There is no really satisfactory adhesive for "Crinothene," although it is possible to use pressure-sensitive adhesives such as "Mystic" for sticking on labels, braids and fringes.

"Rilfoil" is another plastic product very suitable for lampshade making. It is a semi-rigid material and is embossed in two patterns, linen and parchment. It is sold by the yard, at a width of 36 in. The wide range of colours includes white, cream, amber, orange, peach, green, pink and blue. This plastic material is not highly inflammable and is easily cut and shaped to any style of frame. Like "Crinothene," it is very easy to keep clean with warm water and soap flakes, and is very long lasting.

Yet another plastic material suitable for covering lampshades is Acetate. Cellulose Acetate in sheet form is very popular with lampshade makers. This is a plastic material which is manufactured with an almost endless variety of surfaces and colours. Replicas of lace, chintz, leather, etc., are all obtainable in Acetate. This material is not highly inflammable, is very strong, but has one drawback—it cracks very easily if creased. It can be decorated by painting or with transfers. It is best joined by thonging with plastic thongs. Acetate may be cut with a sharp knife or with scissors, or if the surface is scratched with a sharp-pointed tool and the material bent away from the scratch, it will break along the scratch line.

Fabric-covered shades are perhaps the most elaborate and beautiful. A great variety of fabrics is suitable for this purpose. All kinds of silks are very popular, while ginghams, chintz, buckram, crêpes, muslin and lace can all be used with great success in the making of lampshades. They may be used separately or together. Almost any fabric that will permit the passage of light is suitable for covering shades. If it is very thin the shade may be lined with a fine material such as lawn or muslin. When lace or silk net are used they are usually placed over a buckram base, as the materials are not strong enough on their own.

Parchment vellum and stiff art papers are all used extensively for covering lampshades. Amongst this group are to be found old maps, manuscripts and deeds. Real parchments are skins, usually from goats, which have been specially treated so that they are soft, smooth and supple. These are expensive and not easy to come by. The finest qualities are called vellum. However, most arts and crafts stockists list parchment and vellum, and although these are really a form of treated paper, they are excellent for lampshade making, and can be purchased in a variety of colours and mottled patterns. Parchment paper is sold in sheets of various sizes, generally about 50 in. by 20 in., and is obtainable in several qualities. It is not advisable to use the cheapest kinds for lampshade covering, as these crack and discolour very quickly. The price is very economical, and it is one of the most popular lampshade covering materials, lending itself very readily to many methods of decoration. It can be painted with oil colours and spirit colours, or transfers can be used. Parchments and vellums may be enriched by tinting the insides of the shades. This is best done in pink or pale yellow. Designs are easily traced on parchment papers, as the material is translucent, and if the design is placed under the material it can be seen through, and the outlines of the design can then be pencilled in very lightly.

Parchment is obtainable in a wide assortment of colours and also embossed with various surface designs. It can be cut with a sharp knife, a razor blade or scissors.

Thick, good-quality cartridge paper and artists' paper are becoming very popular for making the Scandinavian type of pleated lampshades that have become so fashionable. They can be made translucent by soaking in oil and varnishing, but are mostly used in the natural state.

There are fashions in lampshades as in anything else, and it is now not unusual to see lampshades made from raffia, string, cane, wood veneer, knitted yarns and crochet cottons, and many other materials not usually associated with lampshade covers. The range of materials suitable for covering lampshades is limited only by the individual worker's resourcefulness. Cellophane is often used for shades, when a fancy, not too permanent, covering is required. The Cellophane, which is obtainable in many colours or clear, is used over a cover of stiff paper. A very attractive effect is obtained by using a contrasting coloured paper. The seam of the paper cover is gummed and the cover stitched to the frame. The Cellophane is then pleated or gathered round the shade and held in place by transparent adhesive tape. The shades are completed by adding velvet ribbon over the tape or by making a plait of five strips of Cellophane and sewing these plaits round top and bottom of the shade.

When planning lampshades, colour is very important. The colour of the covering material must tone with the trimmings and also with the general colour scheme of the room in which it is to be used, and it is always advisable to inspect all coloured materials in both day and artificial light. Some coloured materials may look completely different in changes of light.

Most lampshades are joined to the frame by stitching or thonging, and most sewing cottons are suitable for this. Dyed leather thonging can be used but is rather expensive; however, there are many coloured plastic thongings which are sold by the yard and which are very inexpensive, washable and easy to work.

Braids, cords, fringes and fancy trimmings for lampshades are in good supply and in an infinite variety of colours, patterns and widths. Fringes are purely decorative and can be used singly or double—e.g., a fringe of 1¼ in. covered by a contrasting coloured fringe of 1 in. But braids, cords and gimps serve a dual purpose, giving decoration and at the same time providing a way of neatening joints and edges, by covering them.

When string and raffia are used to make shades, the wire frame is first painted a suitable colour, then the raffia or string is wound round and round until the frame is covered. Both these materials can be crocheted or knitted to make covers. Old maps and deeds make some lovely shades, used either alone or with velvet or velour.

Various silk nets can be made into beautiful shades by darning in the forms of a pattern, in coloured silks.

Whatever material is chosen for the cover, the lampshade maker will be well on the way to producing perfect shades if the preparatory work of selecting frames, materials and trimmings is given careful thought.

CHAPTER IV

Making patterns: Importance of accuracy — variation of sizes of sides and panels — treatment of differing materials — main types of foundation frames — popular shapes — patterns for "Empire" covers — curved panel patterns — patterns for fluted lampshade covers — formula for any-size fluted covers.

No matter how carefully a lampshade may be prepared and assembled, unless the pattern used when marking and cutting the covering material to shape is absolutely accurate the lampshade will not be a success. When cutting out the material for covering a shade, it is a great mistake to try to work without a pattern. You will save yourself a great deal of time and avoid wasting materials if a really accurate pattern is made first.

However carefully the wire frames have been made, there may be slight differences in the size of the sides or panels; it is therefore necessary to cut a separate pattern for each panel to allow for these differences, or a main pattern can be used if it is carefully checked against each panel or side for variations of size before the material is cut. Either thick paper or thin card will make a good pattern. Mark round the pattern on the material with a pencil or chalk. A ball-point pen should not be used, as the ink will rub off the pattern on to the covering material and is very difficult to remove. Pattern-making calls for great attention to detail. A very small error can result in a great deal of wasted material, to say nothing of wasted time.

It is a fairly simple matter to make patterns for panelled frames, but not quite so easy to make patterns for one-piece covers or fluted or pleated covers. When commencing to cut a pattern, first consider the material you are going to use. Generally speaking, soft materials are stitched to the frame, and allowance for turning and stitching must be made when cutting out the sides or panels. Stiff materials are cut to the exact size required for thonging or stitching to foundation frames.

There are two main types of lampshade frames—one with supporting side wires which divide the frame into panels, the other consisting of two wire shapes, one for the top and one for the bottom of the shade, which are used when the covering material is stiff enough to support the shade. If the wires of the frame are quite straight and even, it is a simple task to mark out the pattern

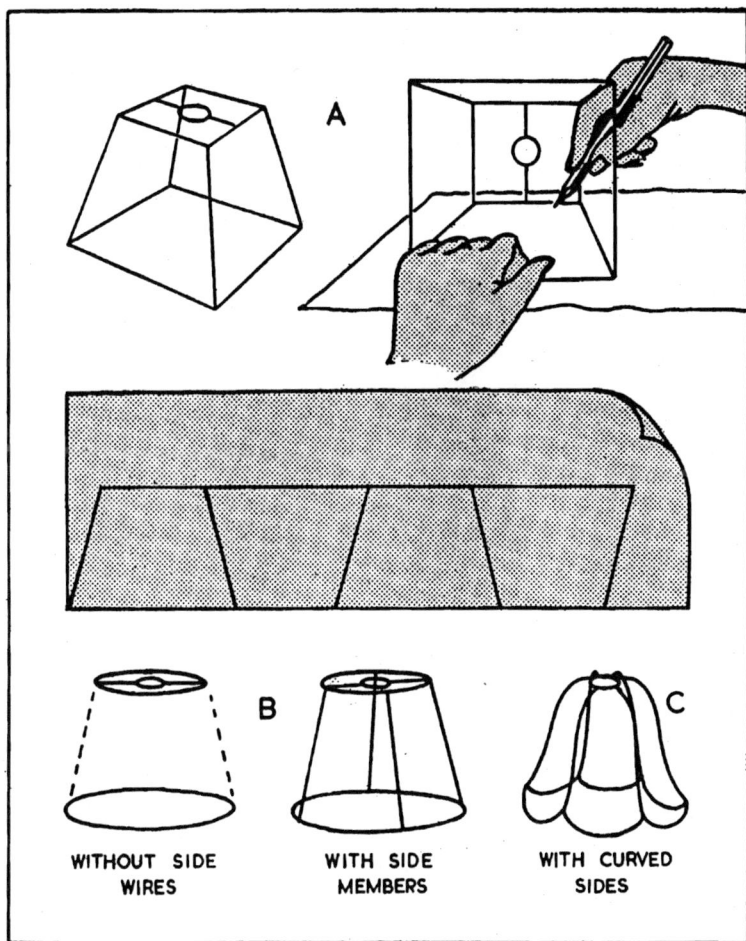

FIG. II. POPULAR FRAME SHAPES

from the frame measurements, but it is more difficult to make an accurate pattern when the wires are curved or round, such as for an "Empire" type shade. The illustration Fig. 11 shows some of the most popular shaped frames.

Fig. 11a is a small square frame suitable for a wall lamp, a chandelier or a very small table lamp, such as is used on a bedside table or dressing table. A pattern for this type of frame can be drawn directly on to a piece of stiff card. Fig. 11 shows how the pattern is drawn to the exact size, and placed on the material so as to avoid any waste. The pattern is the exact size required, and is suitable for use when cutting materials such as parchment, "Crinothene," etc. However, if a soft material is being used, about ¼ in. must be allowed all round the panels for turnings. If several frames are to be covered, a template may be cut in thin plywood or metal. In this case it will be necessary to test the pattern on each panel before starting to cut out the material, so that any variations, no matter how slight, may be allowed for. If chalk is used for marking out your pattern, keep the end well sharpened, as too broad an outline can make quite a considerable difference to the shade.

Fig. 11b shows an "Empire" type frame which can be made in any size, with or without side wires. In either case the covering material is best made in one piece. The diagram Fig. 12 shows how to draw a pattern and may be used for any size frame, ranging from very small candle size to large standard-lamp shades. There are two main points to the diagram—the elevation of the frame which is shown in the diagram in black, and the pattern which you will find heavily outlined. To make a pattern in this way it is necessary to draw an absolutely true elevation of the lampshade frame. Start with a large piece of paper, as it requires quite a lot of space, and at the bottom of the sheet of paper draw the elevation. This means making a drawing of the wire frame as it appears at eye level, and the drawing must be full size. Next draw a vertical line through the centre of the elevation up to the top of the sheet of paper. This line is marked 2—2 in the diagram. Draw a second line by continuing the left side line of the elevation to the top of the sheet; this is marked 3—3 in the illustration.

Now join the top right corner of the elevation with the line 2—2 by drawing an arc with the junctions of 2—2 and 3—3 as the axis. Draw a second arc from the lower right corner of the elevation to line 2—2, again taking the junction of lines 2 and 3 as the axis, draw a quarter circle from the lower left corner of the elevation down to line A below the elevation, and mark off the quarter circle into four equal divisions. Set compasses to any of the four divisions of the quarter circle, and mark off this distance four times from the junction of line 3 and the outer arc. Set the compasses again from the junction of line 3 and the outer arc to the fourth mark previously made on the outer arc, and mark off

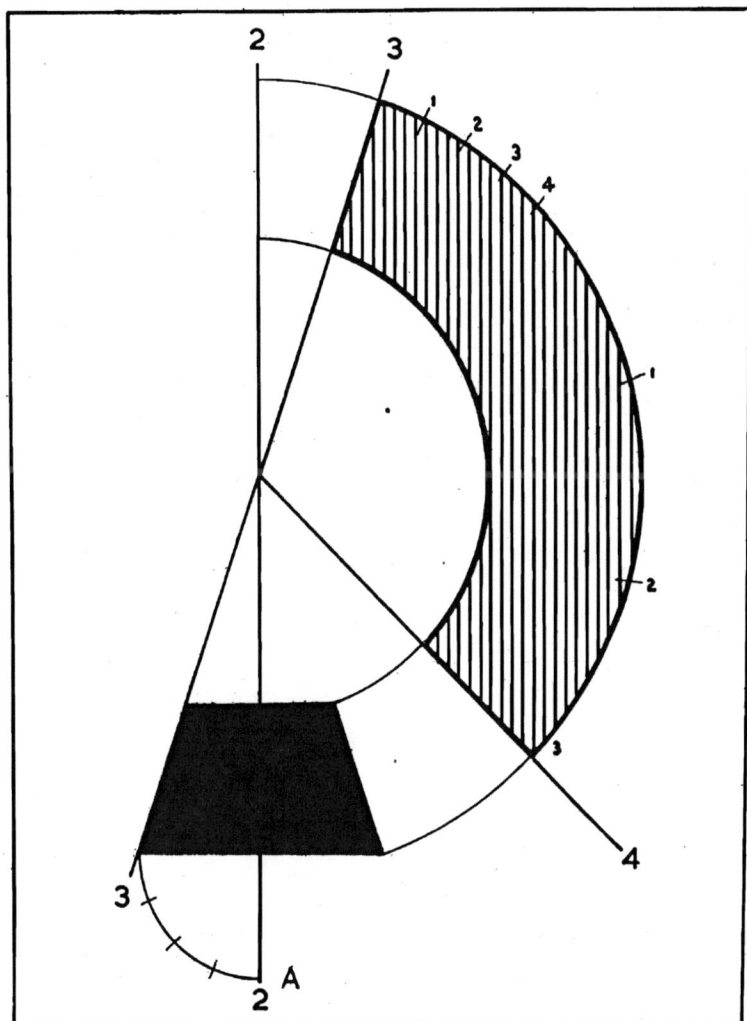

FIG. 12. PATTERN FORMULA

three times. Draw a line from the last mark to the junction of lines 2 and 3; this is line 4 in the diagram. The section of the arc falling between lines 3 and 4, and marked in stripes, is the pattern.

Try the pattern round the wire frame before cutting or marking the material. This method should produce an absolutely accurate

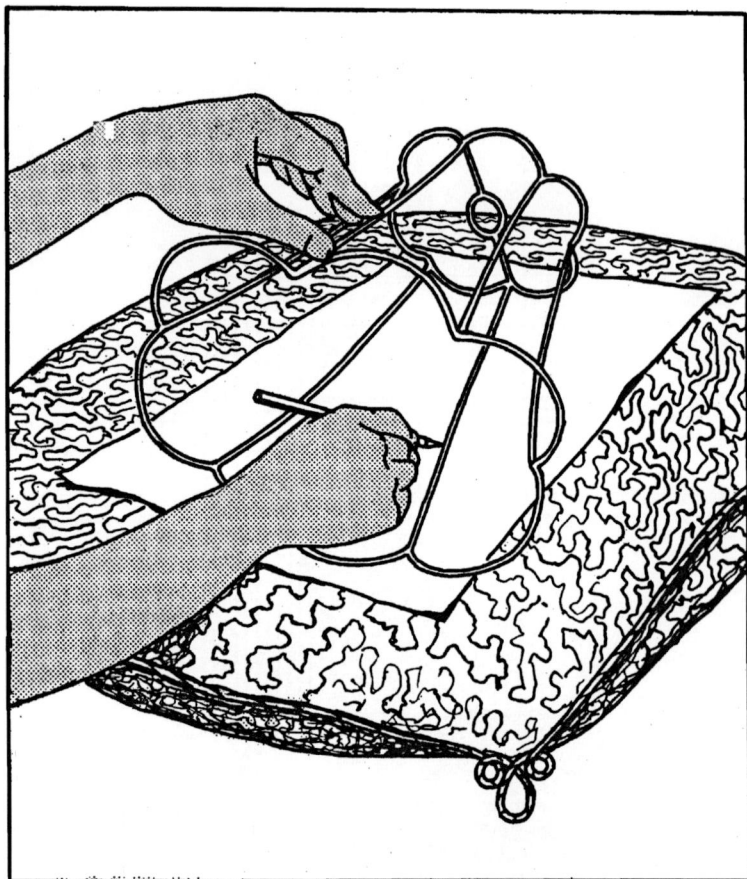

FIG. 13. SHAPED PATTERNS

pattern, but if the frame is to be covered with stiff material, thonged to the frame, allowance must be made for the seam where the two ends meet—about ½ in. is usually sufficient. Patterns are best cut from stiff cardboard, or from wood or metal if you require to cover several shades of a kind. In either case it is essential that they be cut with a very sharp knife or scissors, so that the edges are cut clean.

Patterns for lampshades with curved panels, such as the one illustrated in Fig. 11c, can be made by placing a piece of fairly stiff card or paper on a pillow or cushion. Place a piece of stout paper on top of the card, then press the frame against the paper with enough pressure to make the shaped panel rest firmly on the paper, so that the outline of the panel can be marked in pencil. This is illustrated in Fig. 13. Patterns made by this method must be tried against every panel of the wire frame before cutting the material. Patterns should be cut to the exact size of the panels where a stiff material is to be used for the covering; but if it is intended to use a soft material, an allowance of at least ¼ in. all round the panel will be needed to allow for turnings.

An alternative method for making patterns for curved panels is to place a piece of thin tracing paper over the panel of the frame, and press over the wires until the shape of the panel is impressed on it. Take the paper from the frame and cut round the impression. Try against the wire frame, and if quite accurate place on thin card and trace round it for your pattern.

One of the easiest types of shade for which to cut a pattern is the fluted cover. Fig. 14 gives the measurements for cutting a

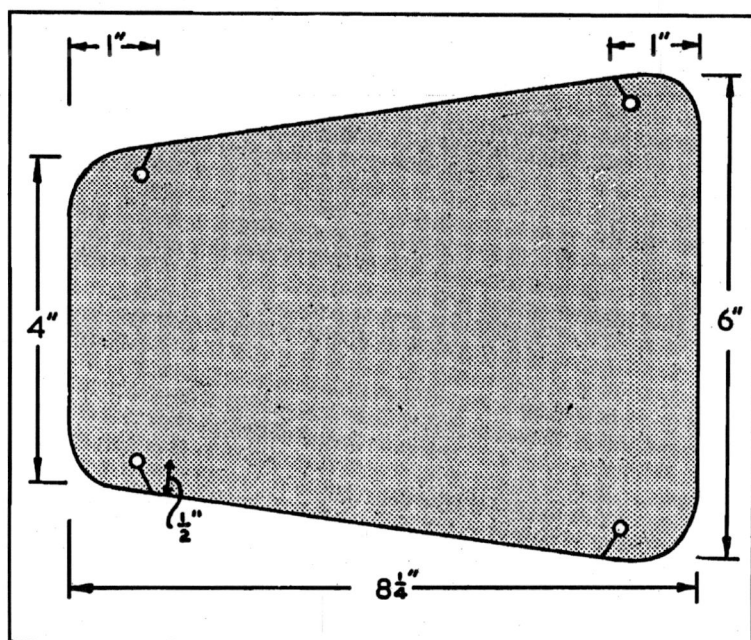

FIG. 14. FLUTED PATTERNS

fluted shade. This type of shade is made on a two-piece wire foundation. The flutes are joined by stitching or stapling. Only a stiff material is suitable for this type of cover. The flutes may be made any size, and any number of flutes may be used for the cover, according to the size of the foundation frame. The fluted shade illustrated has eight flutes. The top ring of the frame is 5 in. in diameter and the bottom ring is 8 in. Cut a pattern from the diagram given and place on the material, reversing for each flute to save wastage of covering material. Cut the flutes and punch four small holes in each, as shown in the diagram. Now make a diagonal cut from the centre of each punched hole to the edge of the flute as shown. The flutes are joined by stitching or by wire staples along a stitch line marked $\frac{1}{4}$ in. from the edge. The wire frames are pressed through the diagonal slits into the punched holes and the edges of the flutes stitched to the frame where they meet. The flutes may be edged with a decorative braid to complete the shade.

The pattern measurements given in Fig. 14 are suitable only for use with a frame of the dimensions given. Patterns for fluted covers for other sizes of frames are quite easy to make. First decide the number of flutes and the depth of shade you wish to make. The cover can consist of more than eight flutes, or if you wish to you can have fewer, although this will cause your flutes to have rather a flat appearance.

Take the bottom ring of the frame and mark this off in equal divisions according to the number of flutes you have decided to have in the shade. Cut a rectangle in stiff card, curve this and hold it against one of the divisions of the base ring. If the curve is too pronounced, trim one side of the card as necessary until you are satisfied that the curve gives a pleasing effect. However, should the curve prove too shallow you will have to cut a wider piece of card. The base of the flute is wider than the top. After cutting away any surplus from the card, round off the corners to neaten the flute, mark the positions where you are going to punch the holes and cut diagonal lines, and the pattern is ready for use.

A fluted shade made with top and bottom rings the same size is very attractive on some lamps, such as a hanging lamp. In this case the pattern for the flutes will be the same size top and bottom. Although this type of pattern is easy to make, a little care in the making of the pattern goes a long way towards making a faultless shade.

CHAPTER V

Simple lampshades: A thonged pendant shade — checking the frame — binding — pattern making — marking and cutting the material — punching the thong holes — thonging — sequence of work — use of plastic thonging. Covering an "Empire" frame — material — inspection — binding the frame — making the pattern — attaching the cover.

THIS chapter deals with the making of two very simple lampshades. The frame of the first one described is illustrated in Fig. 15. It has a square top and a slightly larger square base. The side members are straight, dividing the frame into four panels. This type of frame is obtainable in small sizes suitable for wall lamps or bedside table lamps, up to large standard-lamp sizes. The very small sizes can be had with a fitting known as a "Butterfly" (see Fig. 15). These are shaped wires which fit over the electric-light bulb, and thus enable one to set the shade at any angle.

However, the lampshade described in this chapter is an average-

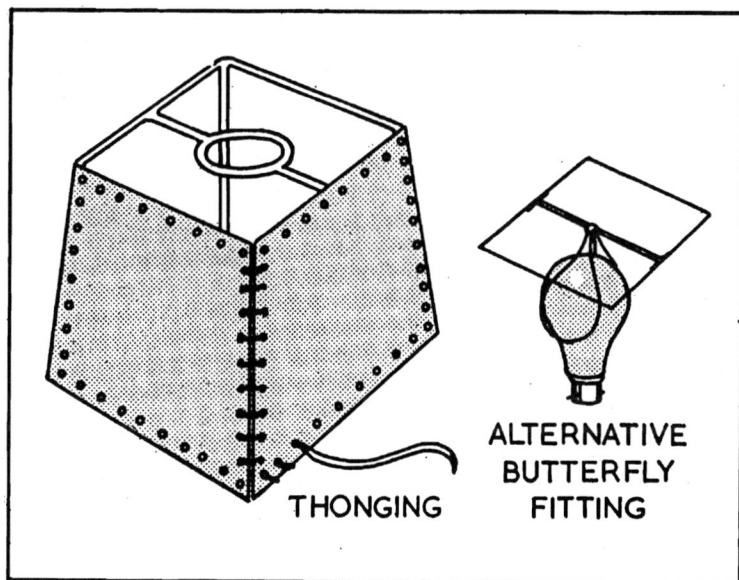

THONGING   ALTERNATIVE
                  BUTTERFLY
                  FITTING

FIG. 15. THONGED COVER

sized pendant with a gimbal at the top, with a thonged cover. When starting to make a shade, the very first thing to do is to examine carefully all the wires, straightening any which may be bent and removing any rust which may be present. Following this simple rule can make a tremendous difference to the shade, as even a very slightly bent wire will prevent your making an accurate panel, while the presence of rust could discolour the inside of the shade.

As this is to be a thonged lampshade, the wires may either be painted to match or contrast with the covering material, or they can be covered with bias binding to match the covering material or the thonging. Bind the frame carefully with tight, slightly overlapping spirals of binding. When you come to a corner, go very carefully to avoid forming bulky joins. Fasten the ends of the bias binding with a fabric adhesive or by sewing. But whichever method is used, make very certain that the binding is securely fastened. Cover all the frame with binding, except the gimbal fitting.

The next stage is to make the pattern. Do not be tempted to save time by marking the shape of the side panels directly on to the material. It is a bad habit to get into when making lampshades, and really it is much more economical in time and covering material to make a well-fitting pattern first. Pattern making is most important, and great care should be paid to this part of the craft.

To make the pattern, take your bound or painted frame and place it on a piece of stiff paper or thin card. With a pencil, mark round one of the side panels. Next cut the panel pattern very carefully. Cut just outside the pencil lines, *not* inside. Test this pattern on each of the four panels. If each of the panels is not completely accurate with the pattern, make a note to make due allowance for these differences when marking and cutting out the covering material. Before marking the covering material it is as well to try the pattern on the material in various ways, to avoid waste in cutting out. It is surprising what a small quantity of material is required to cover a shade if this rule is kept. With straight-panelled frames of this type, the most economical way of placing the pattern is shown in Fig. 16. There is hardly any waste at all. Of course, cover patterns for all frames do not work out so conveniently—such as those with curved panels, for example— but generally time spent at this stage is well worth while.

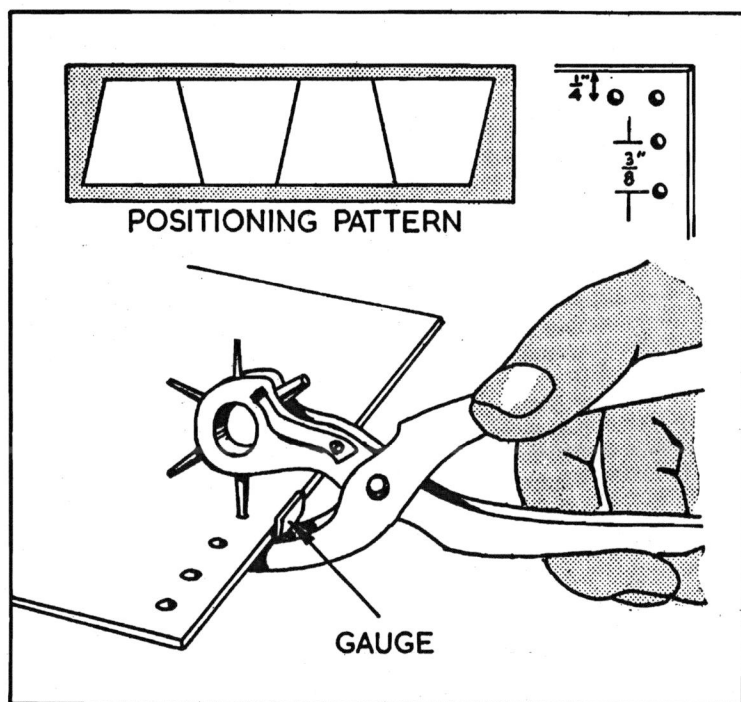

POSITIONING PATTERN

GAUGE

FIG. 16. PLACING PATTERNS

The simple lampshade shape shown can be covered in parchment. This material is obtainable in several qualities and surface patterns and also in several colours. Do not choose the most inexpensive quality: the heavier ones do not tear easily and are, therefore, much easier to work with.

Choose a firm flat surface for use when marking out your pattern. Place the parchment on it and mark round the pattern with pencil. Parchment is easily marked with a lead pencil. Mark out all the four panels, not forgetting to allow for any slight differences in shape or size. Then cut out the material, using a pair of sharp scissors or a razor blade guided by a straight-edge.

Now the next step is to punch the thonging holes all round each of the panels. It is essential for the good appearance of the finished shade that these holes are carefully punched and at equal distances apart. They should be cut at a distance of about $\frac{1}{4}$ in. from the edge and about $\frac{3}{8}$ in. from each other (see Fig. 16).

Choose a punch size which will give a hole big enough to take the thonging but no bigger. Lightly mark the position of the holes on the parchment, or use a gauge such as the one illustrated in Fig. 16. If you are using a six-way revolving-head punch of the type illustrated in Fig. 16, all the panels may be cut at the same time. It is essential that the same number of holes are punched in each panel. There should be no difficulty in punching through the four panels together when the shade is being covered with parchment. The four panels are best held together with a strong paper clip while the holes are punched.

Should the punch being used have become worn and the holes therefore not cut cleanly, place a piece of thin cord over the anvil of the punch, and it will be found that the holes can then be cut quite cleanly.

The panels must now be thonged to the shade. As the shade is being covered with parchment there is no right or wrong side of material; but when using material such as "Crinothene," care should be taken to ensure that the right side of the material is placed on the outside of the shade. The amount of thonging for a lampshade is about three times the total length of the wires. A more attractive appearance results if the width of the thonging is in keeping with the size of the frame. Never use a heavy wide thonging on a small frame, or a dainty narrow one on a large frame.

Commence at one of the top corners by tying one end of the thonging material to one of the wires of the frame. Take two of the panels which have been cut out in parchment, and commencing at the top of the shade secure the sides of both panels to the upright side wires at one of the corners. Pass the thonging from the back of the panels through the second hole down from the top, bring it to the front, and pass it through the coinciding hole of the adjoining panel, over the back of the corner side wire, and through the next hole down in the first panel, as illustrated in Fig. 17.

Continue thonging down to the second hole from the bottom in each panel. Now cut the thonging about ¾ in. from the panel and work the end under the tight thonging inside the lampshade. Release the knot first tied at the top of the shade, cut off any surplus thonging, and tuck the end under inside the tight thonging in the same way. First thong the panels over all the side members of the panels, then thong right round the top of the shade with

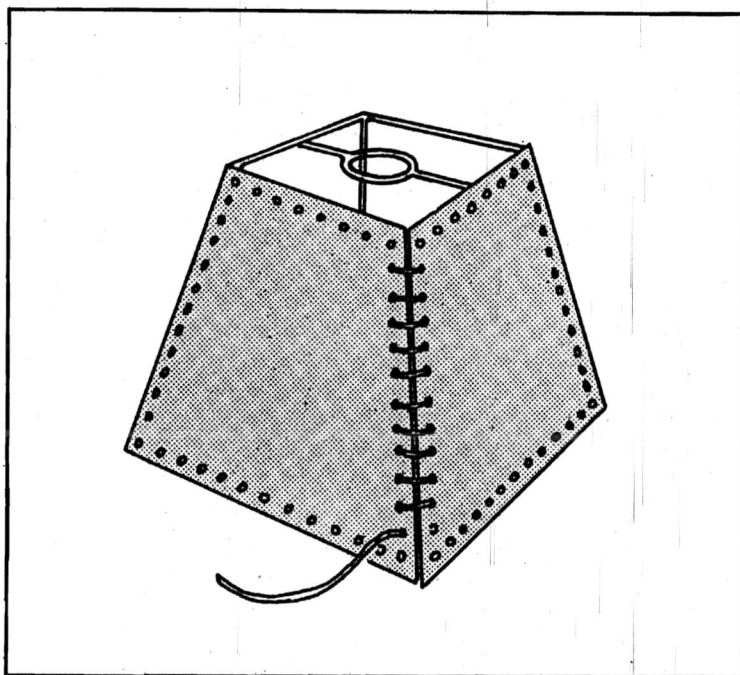

FIG. 17. THONGING

a single length of thonging. Lastly, thong round the bottom of the shade, making sure that all the ends of the thonging are securely tucked out of sight under the thonging inside the shade.

When thonging parchment, care must be taken not to pull the thonging too tight, as if undue strain is placed on the edges of the parchment it may split and break. The thonging need be pulled just tightly enough to hold the material to the frame. Consideration of this becomes very important when using plastic thonging, as some types stretch when warm and shrink as they become cold. The warmth of the hands when handling the thonging may be sufficient to stretch the plastic, and if it is pulled too tightly, when it shrinks it will split the edges of the parchment.

A simple "Empire" type frame without side members is used as the foundation of the next shade described. For this you will need a small ring approximately 5 in. across, fitted with a gimbal, and a larger bottom ring, probably about 8 in. to 10 in. across, without a gimbal. Again, parchment is described as the covering material, but any stiff material is suitable, such as "Crinothene," Acetate, buckram, etc. The material used must be stiff enough to support the shape of the shade, as there are no side members.

To make the lampshade, first inspect the wire rings, making sure that they are not bent out of shape at all and that there is no rust on them. Next, as previously described, paint or bind the rings. If you are binding them, use bias binding wound spirally and slightly overlapping all round each ring, with the exception of the gimbal. Finish off by sticking the end with adhesive or by a few stitches with matching thread. Using the method and diagram shown and described in the chapter on pattern making, mark out in stiff paper or thin card a pattern.

First draw a true elevation of the lampshade at the foot of a large sheet of paper. The elevation must be full size. The width at the top should equal the diameter of the top ring of the frame, and the bottom of the elevation drawn on the sheet of paper should be equal to the diameter of the bottom ring of the shade. As a guide to the suitable height for the shade, add the diameters of the top and bottom rings of the frame and divide the total by two. For instance, if the top ring is 5 in. and the diameter of the bottom ring is 8 in., this gives a total of 13 in., so a suitable height for the shade would be 6½ in. This must be taken as a guide only, and the size of the lampstand, or if pendant the size of the room, should also be considered. After drawing the elevation of the shade, draw a straight line extending the left side of the elevation. Draw a second line vertically through the elevation in the centre. From the axis where these lines meet draw an arc from the bottom left corner of the elevation to the top of the paper. To complete the pattern outline, take the largest ring and roll it along the arc. Mark the ring with chalk at the starting-point, and also mark the paper at the starting-point. Mark again when the mark on the frame reaches the line. From that point draw a line to the axis. This is illustrated in Fig. 12.

Place it on the parchment (with this type of frame there is bound to be some wastage in cutting, but the pieces can probably be utilized to make a panelled shade). Make an allowance for overlapping seam. Test the cover on the frame, and if you are certain it is an accurate fit, mark out the thonging holes all round the bottom and top edges.

Commence the thonging at the top edge by tying the thonging material to the wire, then work round the top ring, finishing the ends as was described for the previous shade, by putting them neatly under the thonging inside the shade. Now join the side seam, which may either be stuck with adhesive or, if preferred, holes can be punched and threaded through with the thonging. Then thong in the same way round the bottom of the shade. Make sure that the thonging lies in the same direction round the bottom ring as it does round the top one.

These two frames are the simplest ones to cover, but there is great variety in the manner in which they can be covered, and when covered in fabric and daintily trimmed they look anything but simple. The lampshade maker is well advised to explore and learn thoroughly the many ways in which these two shapes can be covered, before attempting the more difficult, curved types of frame.

CHAPTER VI

Lampshades with stitched covers: Bed-lamp shade — preparation — choice of material — making patterns — stitching — decoration. Another bed-lamp shade — inspecting the frame — binding — sewing — attaching net frill. Standard-lamp shade — curved and rounded panels — checking the frame — binding — thonging and stitching — decoration.

AFTER making simple thonged shades, the worker can progress to other kinds. The next type of lampshade described has a stitched cover, and this is no more difficult to make than a thonged shade. For this type of lampshade one of the plastics such as "Crinothene" or "Rilfoil" can be used. The shade chosen to illustrate this method is a bed-lamp shade, which is made on one of the standard-style frames which are obtainable from all handicraft dealers.

The preparation for making a stitched cover is much the same as for thonged covers. Commence by examining the frame for rust and bends in the wire. Slight rust can be removed by rubbing hard with a pad of newspaper, and do not be tempted to leave the rust on the frame, as it may come through the cover later and ruin the shade. With stitched covers it is always necessary to bind the frames with bias binding. It is not enough to paint them, as the stitching is done through the binding and it is then finally covered with gimp. This serves two purposes—it covers the joints in the shade and serves to decorate the lampshade.

The lampshade illustrated in Fig. 18 is a shade for a bed-lamp, and in making it there is one extra point to be considered. It is a common fault amongst lampshade workers to make small lampshades with the top completely covered in. This is a bad fault, as in these small shades the bulb is of necessity nearly touching the shade, and the heat from it, in an enclosed space, will cause the covering material to scorch, singe or melt, according to the type being used.

To overcome this, the shade must be designed to allow a small part at the back or top to be left open, to allow the hot air generated by the heat from the bulb to escape. In the case of the lampshade illustrated, it is obvious that the top must be covered in one piece with the front, then the two sides. The part between the two wires at the back, just below the hook, is left uncovered, thus leaving a space for the escape of the heat.

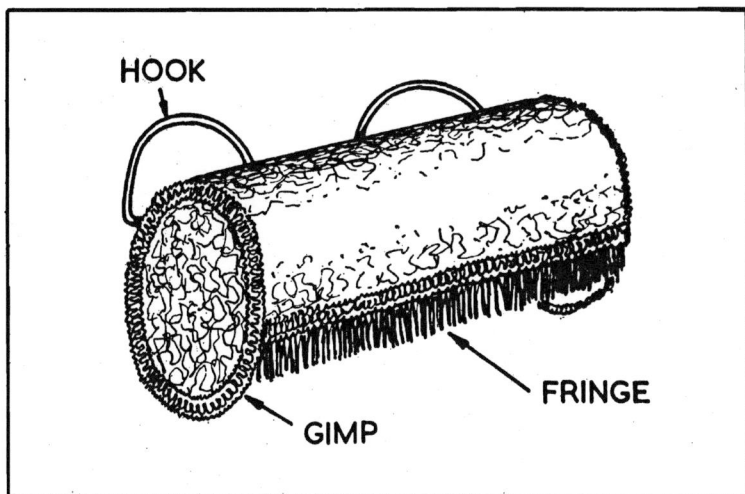

FIG. 18. BED-LAMP

To make the lampshade, first inspect all the wires and then bind the frame as previously described. Cover all the wires except the gimbal ring.

As this lamp is to be used on a bedhead, choose a soft, restful colour for the "Crinothene," something which will suggest comfortable relaxation—warm peach or amber, decorated with gimp and a small fringe. The parts of this frame are quite small, and if the worker has off-cuts of "Crinothene" at hand it may be possible to combine two colours, one for the top piece and one for the side pieces.

Make the patterns after inspecting and binding the frame with bias binding. In this case it will be quite a simple matter to make patterns for the three pieces—one for the top, which reaches from the front wire to the top back wire by the hook, and two circles to fit the ends, which are closed in completely. Take careful measurements and cut out in stiff card or thick paper—even with such simple shapes as these it is inadvisable to mark directly on to the covering material. Try the patterns against the frame to ensure that they are accurate, then place the patterns on the material, mark round them with chalk, and cut the parts neatly to shape.

Commence stitching the cover to the frame with one of the side

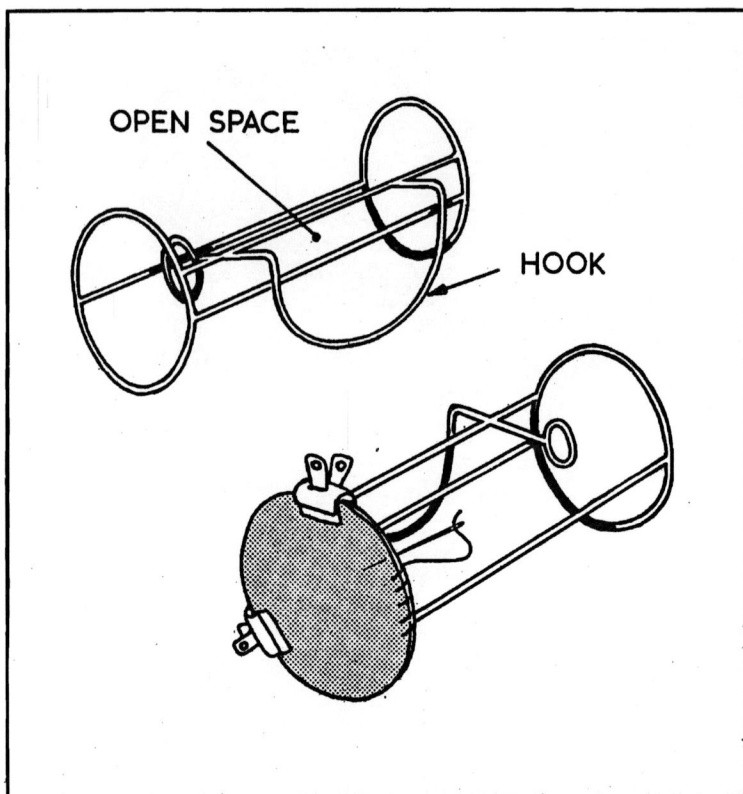

FIG. 19. SEWING " CRINOTHENE "

panels. Place the panel on the bound wire, and with a needle threaded with strong matching cotton stitch the panel to the bias binding, and stitch right round the edge of the circle. When sewing "Crinothene" care must be taken not to allow the covering material to move, and to prevent this one or two paper clips can be used, as shown in Fig. 19, to keep the panel in place. Every care must be taken not to buckle the panel while stitching it in place, and it is at this stage that the value of cutting accurate patterns becomes apparent. If pattern making has not been absolutely accurate the panel may turn out to be a little too small or a little too large, and "Crinothene", which has little elasticity, may not stretch to fill gaps caused by poor pattern making.

The thread used for sewing the cover to the bound wires should match the covering material, for although it will not show on the outside it will be seen from the inside.

"Crinothene" is quite easy to sew with a medium fine sewing needle, but "Rilfoil," which may be used as an alternative covering, requires a slightly larger needle to go through easily. The stitch line with both these materials should be about $\frac{1}{8}$ in. to $\frac{1}{4}$ in. in from the edge of the material, but it may be a little more, and it is best not to make more than eight stitches to the inch. If more than eight stitches are made to each inch, it may weaken the material at the edges. As "Crinothene" is fairly easily pierced with a sewing needle, there is no need to punch stitch holes, though this can be done if desired—with a sharp-pointed bradawl —before commencing stitching.

After the first side panel has been stitched into place on the lampshade frame, fit the other round panel to the opposite end and stitch it firmly into place.

Care should be taken while stitching not to pull the cotton too tightly, as a strong cotton may tear the covering material if pulled too tightly. With the ends attached fit and stitch the main panel, which reaches from the front wire over the top of the frame to the first wire at the back. This completes the actual stitching of the frame, which will need decorating to finish.

As this lamp is for use in a bedroom, the decoration can be a little more fancy than those of a living-room lampshade, and the choice of colour will depend largely upon the room in which the bed-lamp is to be used. The lampshade illustrated is decorated with gimp and fringe. When making this particular shade it will be necessary to stitch the fringe along the bottom of the shade first. One piece of fringe may be used. The gimp is attached next. This should be of a suitable colour to tone with the covering material, and it should be wide enough to fold over the stitched seams of the shade and completely cover the joins and stitches. Take a length of gimp and place it over one corner of the lampshade. Using cotton of a suitable colour, commence stitching at the top of the shade and work downwards, sewing the gimp neatly and firmly in place. Stitch gimp along the two long edges, then sew it round the two ends. When stitching gimp, sew through the "Crinothene" and the bias binding, and sew along both edges of the gimp. Do not make the mistake of sewing over the wires inside the frame, as this spoils the look of the finished shade.

The next shade to be described is also for a bed-lamp, and this lampshade consists of three panels and a back piece, as illustrated in Fig. 20. The gimbal is at the top of the shade.

The style of shade is very suitable for using two colours of covering materials. The back and front panels can be done in cream and the petal-shaped panels in deep rose. The lampshade would be best trimmed with a box-pleated frill of double net in a matching rose colour.

As in previous instructions, commence by carefully inspecting the wire frame for any faults in the construction and for rust. It should be emphasized here that these frames are not usually faulty—indeed, if bought from a reputable firm they are generally very accurate and completely free from rust; but it may some-times happen that corresponding panels vary in size by a very slight degree. Therefore it can save a great deal of wasted material

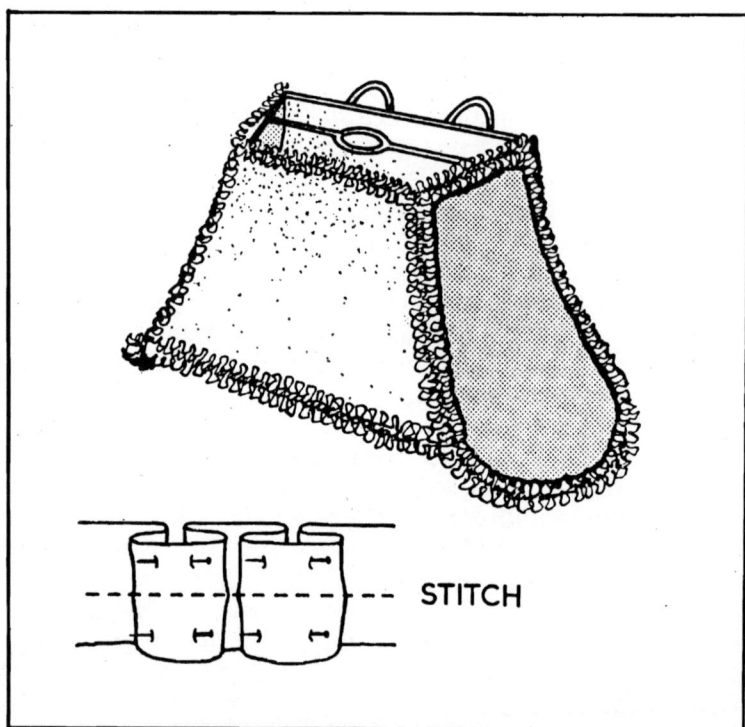

STITCH

FIG. 20.   ANOTHER BED-LAMP

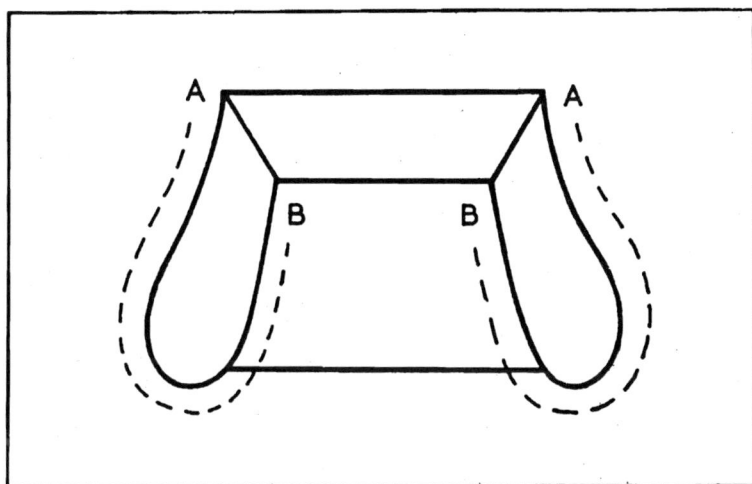

FIG. 21.   DECORATING A BED-LAMP

if this simple check is made when commencing to make a lamp-shade.

Bind the wire frame with bias binding. In this shade, as the two main panels are rose, the binding should be of the same colour. When making a two-coloured frame it is usually best to match the binding to the predominating colour.

Take time and trouble over binding the frame to ensure that it is tight and smooth, with no lumpy corners, then make the pattern. As the panels of this shade are covered at the ends, though still flat across, the best way of marking the pattern to shape is to use the frame itself. Rub white chalk over the bound wires on the outside of the shade, then press a panel on brown paper or cardboard.

Commence by stitching the back panel to the frame; in this particular shade the top is left open and the back is completely filled in. Stitch the front panel to the frame, then attach the two petal-shaped panels.

To make the frill, two lengths of net about three times the total length of wires to be covered (*e.g.*, the measurements of the two petal panels, plus right round the top of the shade, plus across the front wire) will be required (see Fig. 20). Place the pieces of net one on top of the other and pin into box pleats right along

the length of the net, as illustrated in Fig. 20. Stitch through the
middle of the pleats, remove the pins, and stitch or stick with
white adhesive a piece of the frill across the bottom front wire,
then a piece round each petal panel from A to B, as shown in
Fig. 21. To finish, put the remaining piece around the top. If
additional decoration is required, add a very narrow gimp down
the centre of the frill.

The next stitched lampshade, shown in Fig. 22, is for a large
standard lamp and is slightly more difficult to make than those
previously described, because of the curved and rounded panels
and because, being a large frame with many panels, it is a little

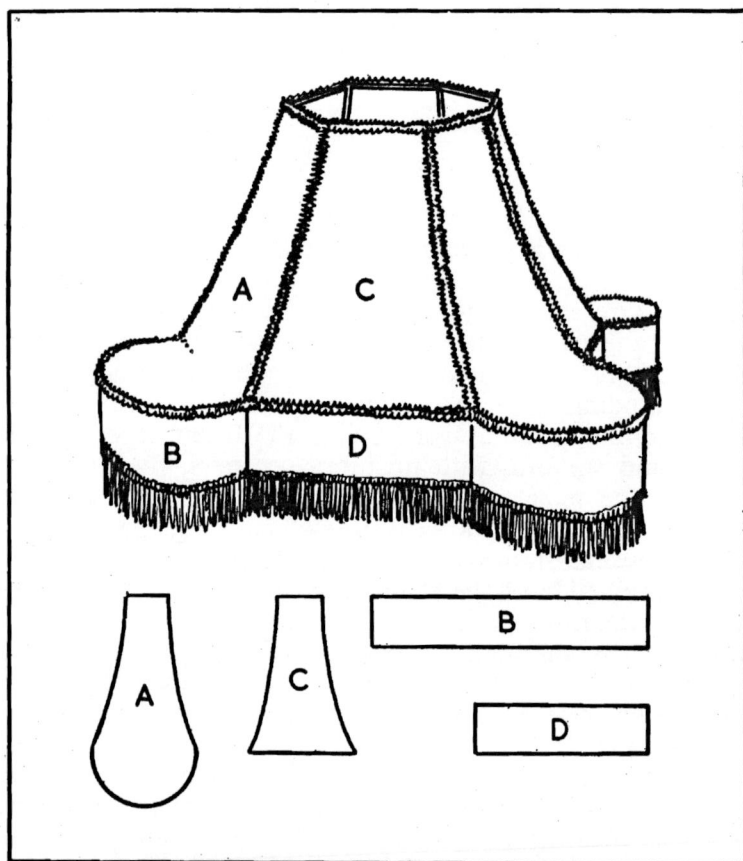

FIG. 22.   STANDARD LAMPSHADE

more difficult to handle while making. There are four different shapes in the panels, and the shade is made up of sixteen panels altogether. In Fig. 22 the panel shapes are marked A, B, C and D.

Commence, as always in lampshade making, by checking the wire frame. In a shade of this size it is advisable to go further and check the joints in the wire frame. It is unlikely that there will be any fault in them, as the best manufacturers make their frames with strong, well-finished spot-welded joints.

Next bind all the wires of the frame with bias binding. In a many-panelled shade such as this it will take thought and care to avoid lumpy corners. The best sequence of work will be to bind down the curved side and down the small upright wires, finishing each end with a few stitches. Continue by binding right round the top wire, next right round the two bottom wires. In this way you will avoid going over the same corner too many times.

In the shade illustrated both thonging and stitching have been employed. The upright sides of the panels are thonged, and the top and bottom edges stitched and covered with gimp. The thonging used and the gimp should be an exact match in colour.

After covering the frame with bias binding, place it against a sheet of strong paper and place both paper and frame on a soft cushion or pillow, press the frame well down into the cushion, and the paper will then take on the shape of the panel (see Fig. 13). Draw round the outline of the panel on the paper. Cut the pattern out and test it against the other panels of the same shape. Make patterns for the other panel parts in the same way.

Punch thonging holes along the edges of the panel to be thonged, making certain that the holes in neighbouring panels coincide. Thong the panels into position, then stitch along the tops of all the panels and along the two bottom wires.

Cover all the stitched edges with gimp, either sewn or stuck on. If a fringe is required on these large frames, try a double one, made by using two lengths of fringe each a different colour and length. For instance, have a fringe matching the "Crinothene," about 3 in. deep, and another fringe about 2 in. deep to match the gimp. Use the small fringe over the longer one, so that the two colours mingle.

CHAPTER VII

Fabric-covered lampshades: Materials — binding the frame — making the pattern — covering the frame — trimming. A bowl-shaped shade. Another method of making fabric-covered lampshades. Novelty methods — using lace or net over stiff paper.

THIS chapter deals with the making of fabric-covered lampshades. Fabric lampshade covers are quite easy to make if the directions are carefully followed and the correct sequence of work is observed.

There are very many fabrics suitable for covering lampshades— in fact, any material that does not completely block out light can be used as a covering, but loosely woven materials are difficult to use, as they do not hold the stitches very well.

There are several methods by which fabric lampshades are made, and it is a matter of choice which method is adopted. In some cases the shape of the frame will indicate a particular method.

When making a fabric lampshade the panels may be covered separately, or several panels may be covered together, or again the cover can be made in one piece for attachment to the frame.

The lampshade shown in Fig. 23 illustrates a method by which fabric covers can be made to fit simply shaped frames of any size. The illustration shows a medium-sized pendant shade in which all the panels curve inwards. Usually it will be found that lampshade frames with concave panels (inward curving) are generally more suitable for covering with fabric than are frames with convex (outward curving) panels.

As when making other shades, the wire frame must be checked carefully and any bent wires straightened out. Rust spots can be removed by rubbing with a pad of newspaper, or if very bad, with emery paper. Check for any broken joints, and when this has been done bind the frame with bias binding in the manner previously described. The binding may alternatively be done with strips of the covering material, and if this is done cut strips of material about 1 in. in width. Fold over and press one edge of the strips; it is not necessary to fold over both edges, as the other raw edge is covered by the overlapping folded edge while binding the frame. If the covering material is thick it will be found best

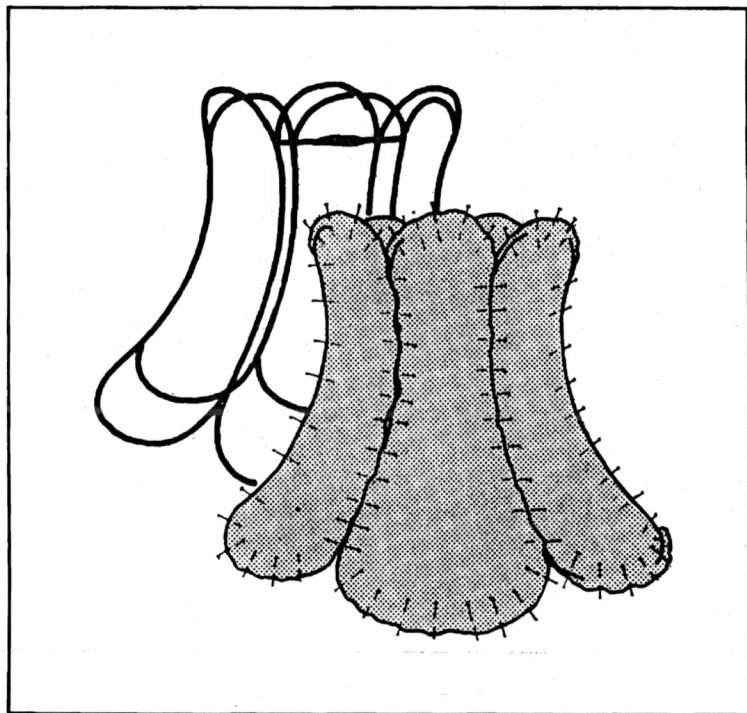

FIG. 23. FABRIC COVER

to use bias binding; but whatever binding is used, the frame must be bound tightly and carefully, avoiding lumps and awkward joins, as these may show under a fabric cover.

When covering a shade in the manner shown in Fig. 23, first bind all the side wires, then bind round the top and finish round the bottom. When making fabric-covered lampshades it is most important to remember that the covering material must *always* be used on the cross or bias, so that the stretch is even in all directions. For first attempts at lampshade making choose an easy-to-handle material, such as washing satin or one of the cotton crêpes.

Fig. 24 illustrates a very quick and easy way of covering a lampshade. This is not strictly a professional method, but it gives very good results. This method is not suitable for all shapes of frames, but works very well on those with several straight panels. The shade illustrated is one of the ready-made frames which can be obtained from most handicraft dealers. It has a base of about 12 in. diameter and is suitable as a pendant or a table lamp. To cover this frame you will require a piece of material about 27 in. square; cut this diagonally across to form two triangles. This cover is made of two pieces which are joined with two side seams.

Make a rough paper pattern of half the frame. The pattern need not be exact, as adjustments can be made when stitching the cover. Lay the pattern on the two triangles of material, which should be placed together, and tack very carefully down both sides of the pattern and the pieces of material. Take the material and pattern and slip over the frame. Pin down the side seams, keeping the material very taut (see Fig. 24). Remove the cover from the frame, and machine-stitch or back-stitch along the side seams about ¼ in. away from the pins. This is done to allow for french seams. Cut away all surplus material from the sides only, but do not cut the top or bottom of the material.

A french seam is useful in making lampshades, as it will hide raw edges, and materials which are likely to fray will be protected at the seam edges. After machining down the seam on the right side of the material (about ¼ in. from the pins marking the position of the finished seam), trim off any surplus material wrong side out, and pin or tack the seam, making sure that the raw edges of the first seam are folded inside the second line of stitching, and sew along the seam at the position of the first set of pins.

It is very necessary that the covering should be taut on the frame, and at this stage try the covering over the frame again and make adjustments necessary. When the side seams are satisfactory, put the covering back on the frame right side out, and pull it well down on the frame. Pin top and bottom of material to the bound wires at top and bottom of the shade, pulling very tightly before pinning to ensure that the material is completely free from wrinkles. Turn the material over the wires and with matching cotton stitch down all along, taking each stitch right over the wire. Cut away any surplus material. The shade is now ready for the trimming, and this particular lampshade is simply decorated with narrow gimp around top and bottom. Place the gimp so that it comes just over the edge of the wires and covers the stitches. This is the simplest form of fabric-covered shade.

The next method described is rather more professional and is used for every variety of shaped frame. To illustrate this method the making of a bowl shade to hang from the ceiling is described. These bowl-shaped frames are hung close to a ceiling to give a very pleasant diffused light. If expense is no object this type of frame may be covered in one piece, but it will require a very large

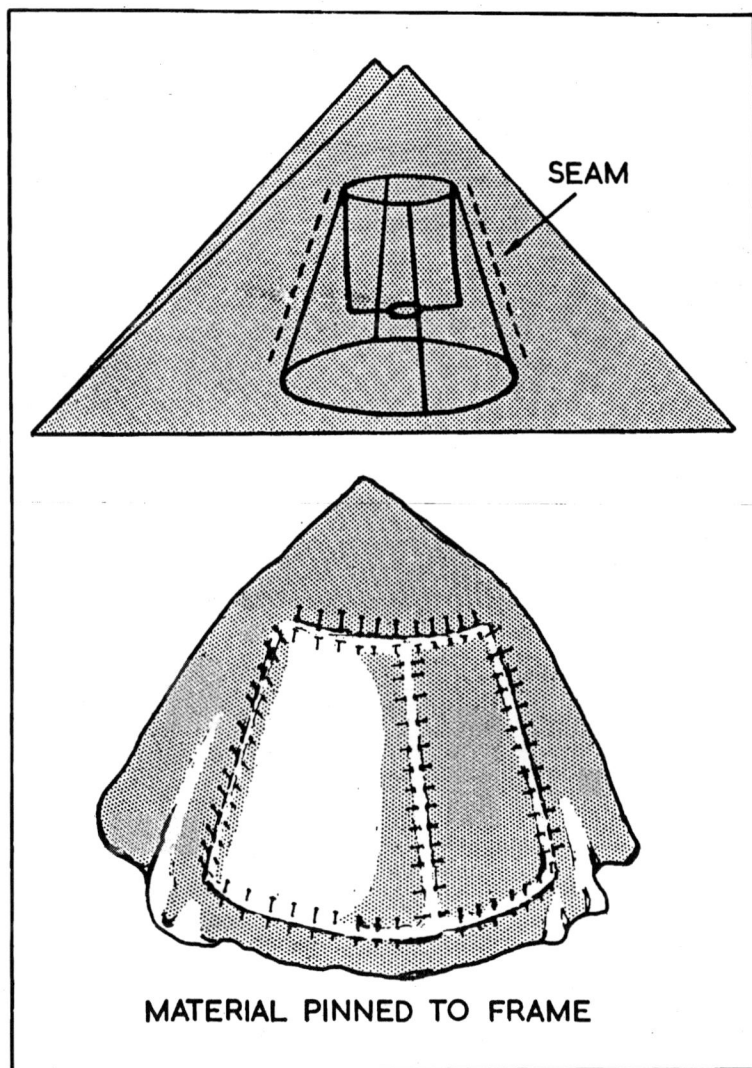

SEAM

MATERIAL PINNED TO FRAME

FIG. 24. QUICK AND EASY METHOD FOR FABRICS

piece of material to get it on the true bias, and it will be found more economical to cover it in two pieces.

The illustration Fig. 25 shows how the material is fitted over half the foundation by pinning it to the tape-bound edges of the frame. Commence by folding over one corner of the material to form a triangle which can then be cut off, to ensure that the material is used on the bias. This trimmed corner should be pinned parallel with the top of the frame when the cover is

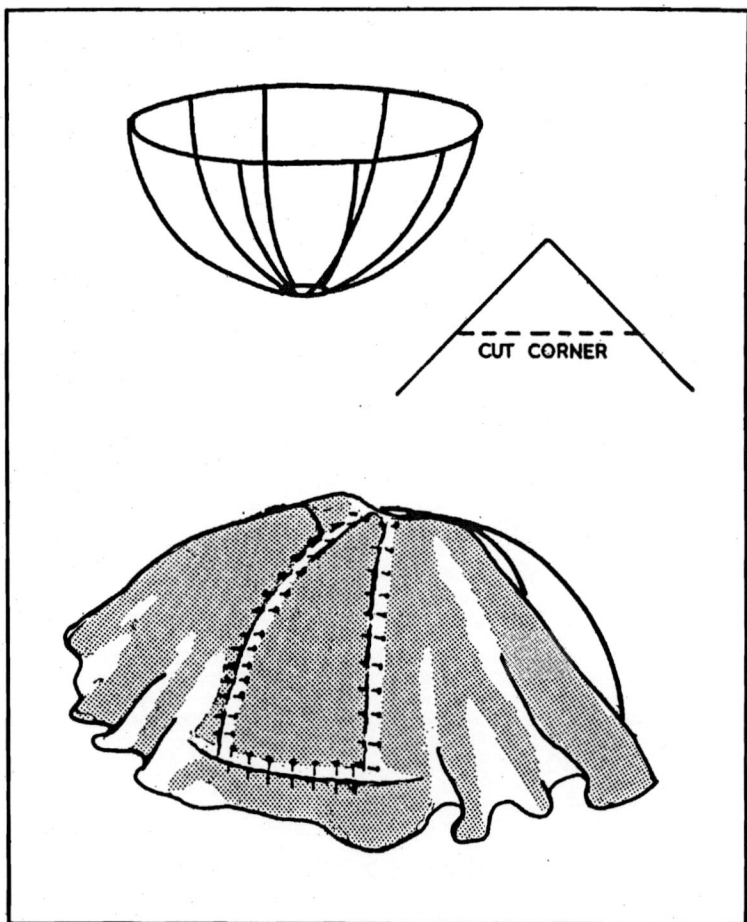

CUT CORNER

FIG. 25. FITTING MATERIAL

commenced. Using small steel pins, pin the material to the top
wire of the frame, as shown in the illustration, commencing at
the centre panel, then move to the bottom of the panel and pin
that to the bound wire, keeping the material very taut, and using
plenty of pins so that the material is held firmly and securely.
The pins at top and bottom should all be vertical. After fastening
the material at top and bottom, pin along one side edge, fastening
the pins through the material and the binding over the wire frame.
Pin all along one side very firmly, then pull and stretch the
material well so that there are no wrinkles and it is really taut
over the panel, then pin the second side very firmly to the frame.

Be generous with the use of pins, and place them all hori-
zontally at the side edges. After pinning all sides, commence at
a top corner, pulling the material tightly to shape, remove one
pin at a time, then replace it after tightening the material. Work
all round the panels in this way, removing a pin, pulling the
material tight, and replacing the pin in position. Only by giving
attention to this part of the work can you get a perfectly smooth
cover with no sags or wrinkles and the strain even in all directions. After stitching and pinning the first panel, move round to
the next one and repeat the tightening process. Pin the top first,
then the bottom, next the side edge. Starting again at the top
corner, remove the pins one by one, pull the material taut and
replace the pins. When this has been done all round the second
panel, go on to the panel on the other side of the first panel and
repeat the process.

When the three panels have been covered and the material is
evenly stretched and firmly pinned over the wires, trim away any
surplus material to within $\frac{1}{8}$ in. to $\frac{1}{4}$ in. of the pins. Next thread
an ordinary sewing needle with cotton or strong sewing silk of a
colour to match the covering material. Sew along the top edge,
first turning the material over, and sew through the folded
material to the bound wire. Oversew the edges and remove the
pins one at a time as progress is made. Never take out more than
one or two pins at a time, or the tension of the material will relax.
Sew firmly along the top edge, then down the left edge, removing
only one or two pins at a time. Sew up the right side edge. While
oversewing the edges of the cover, trim and neaten the edge as
you go along. It is not necessary to sew along the other two wires
dividing the three panels, and the pins holding these two wires
may be removed after all the edges have been stitched.

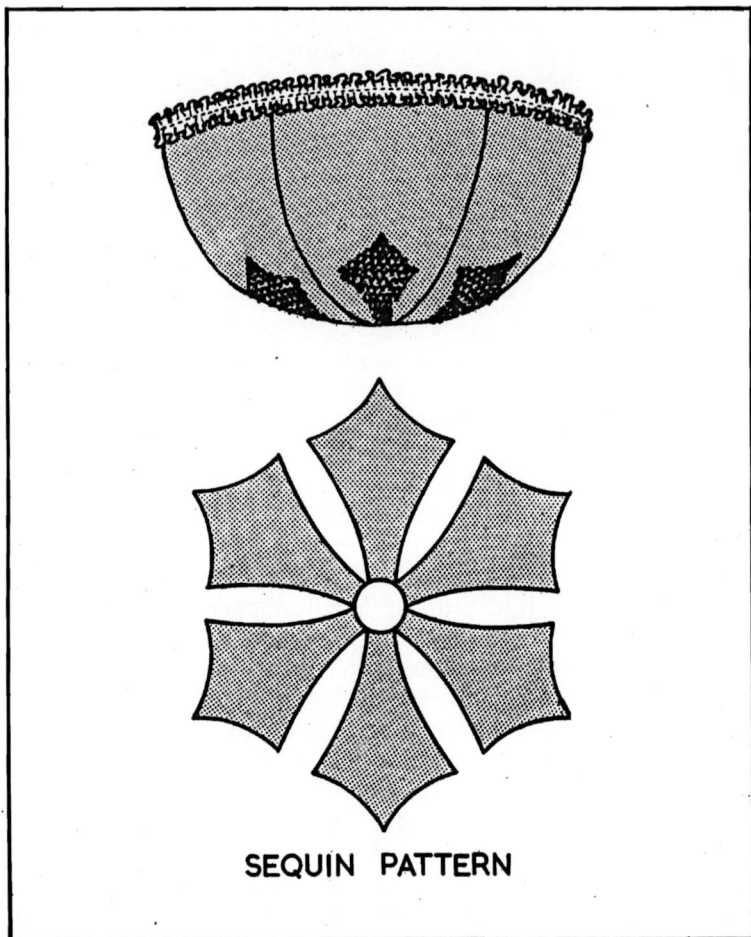

SEQUIN PATTERN

FIG. 26.　DECORATING SHADES

The second half of the cover is made in the same way, by stretching the material on the bias over the remaining three panels, pinning round each panel as the work progresses to remove all sags, wrinkles and creases, and lastly stitching the edges to the tape-bound wires of the frame. It will be seen from this description of covering a lampshade how very important it is to bind the frame carefully and firmly. If the binding is loose in any place it will not stand up to the strain of the material, and the cover will develop sags where the weaknesses of the binding are.

When the covering has been completed the inside should be carefully inspected and any raw edges that show inside should be trimmed, but if the work has been carefully done from the beginning, and the edges of the material trimmed as they are oversewn, there should not be any ragged edges visible inside the frame.

If a thin material is being used to cover the frame it may need a lining, and this, if required, is fairly easy to fit. It is put into place in the same way as the cover, by stretching, pinning, tightening, trimming and stitching the lining material over the bound wires, exactly as for the cover, but in this case work from the inside of the shade. To save making bulky seams at the side wires when working the lining, make only two panels at a time, and so arrange the seams that they run along the side wires of the frame, to which the covering material will not be stitched.

The bowl-type frame illustrated could be trimmed in several ways—it could have gimp stitched along all the edges, with a tassel falling from the centre, or it could have ruching along the top wire edge and a gathered rosette arranged at the centre point where the wires meet.

The lampshade in Fig. 26 has, however, been decorated in a more ambitious style. The covering material is deep cream satin, and a rather wide ruching of the same material has been stitched along the top wire. Starting from the centre point, a pattern in gold-coloured sequins has been built up with a point going up each pattern—the illustration shows how the pattern is built up. Each sequin is stitched to the cover with matching thread, and one tiny glass bead is stitched to the centre of the sequins at the same time.

Yet another method of making fabric-covered lampshades is shown in Fig. 27, and this method is one usually adopted by professional lampshade makers when covering shades with many curves and panels, and for large standard shades where it is difficult to keep the material tight while working large areas. It takes more time than the other methods described, and requires skilful handling to avoid making too many bulky seams, but if well done it produces a perfect shade.

Commence by inspecting the wire frame, as this is the basis of the finished work. It cannot be stressed too often that you cannot build a perfect cover on a frame which is not straight and free from rust marks. Bind the wires as has been described, taking care over the corners to avoid bulk. Cut a pattern for each

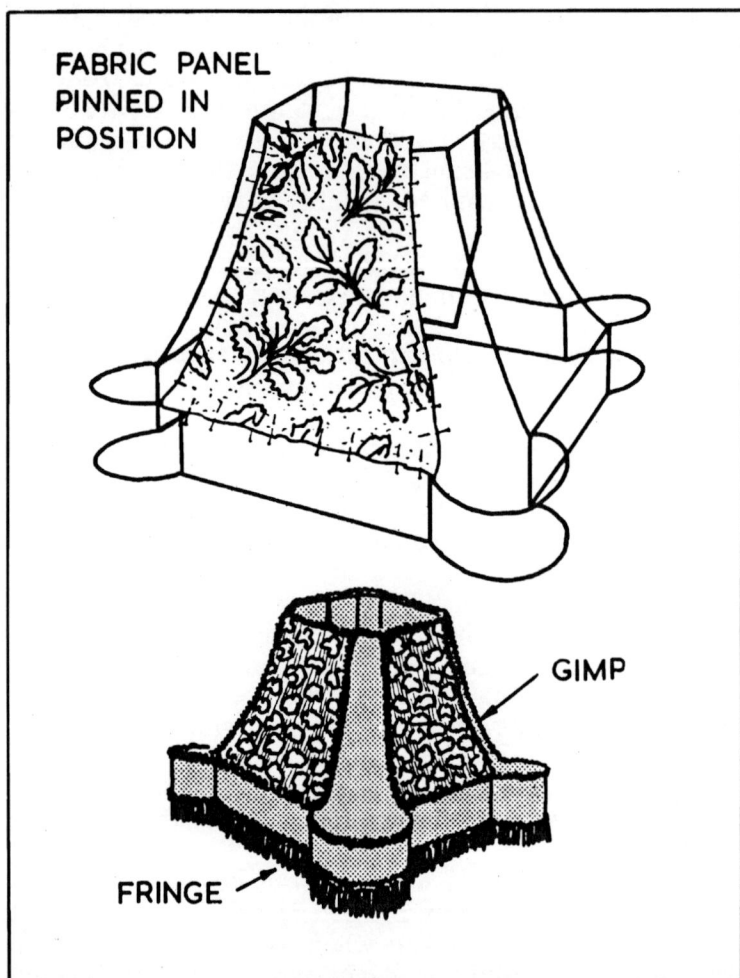

FABRIC PANEL
PINNED IN
POSITION

GIMP

FRINGE

FIG. 27.   METHOD OF DECORATING

separate panel of the frame and place the pattern pieces on the
material, making quite sure that each piece is on the true bias of
the material. Check this very carefully, as faults cannot be
remedied once the material is cut—making a mistake in a large
cover of a costly material could be a very expensive business.
Cut the material to shape, allowing a good inch to an inch and
a half all round each pattern piece.

Take one panel at a time and pin the material to the wires bordering the panel, as shown in Fig. 27. Pin at the top first, then the bottom, and finally at the side wires. Make absolutely certain that the material is quite taut and the strain evenly distributed in all directions, then cut off any surplus material along one edge to within about a quarter of an inch.

Using a thread of matching colour and a fairly fine sewing needle, stitch the material to the binding round the wire, turning the edge under with the needle and removing the pins one at a time until the panel has been completed. While stitching trim off the surplus material at each edge. Do not take a short cut and trim all the edges of a panel before commencing the stitching, as the material will fray when pulled taut.

Continue in this way, completing one panel at a time, until all the shade is covered. If the work is neatly done there should be no raw edges visible from the inside of the shade, but if the material is thin or of a dark colour and a lining, perhaps in pale pink, is wanted, it can be made in exactly the same way and sewn in from the inside of the frame. This should be done first before the covering material is stitched on. These shades are decorated in any of the ways described in the chapter on decorating lampshades at the end of the book. The one illustrated has the seams covered with fancy gimp, and a fringe hangs from the lower wire. Stitch the fringe under the lower wire, then stitch the gimp over the wire.

Besides these orthodox methods of covering shades with fabrics there are several novelty ways in which attractive shades may be made. One of these is to use thin material, lace or net, over a stiff paper. Fig. 28 illustrates a table-lamp shade that is very effective and very simple to make. Two lampshade-frame rings of the same size are required, and 8-in. rings were used for the one shown. The bottom ring should have a gimbal fitting. The top ring (without the gimbal) should be bound all round with bias binding and the second ring (with the gimbal) should be bound with the exception of the gimbal. Make a circular pattern to cover the top ring, cut this out in stiff white drawing paper and stitch the circle of paper to the ring. This must be done carefully or the paper may tear. Now cut a strip of paper about 6 in. wide and the length of the circumference of the ring plus $\frac{1}{2}$ in. for the seam. Gum the strip of paper into a tube and when dry stitch one end of this tube to the ring which is covered with paper.

c

FIG. 28.   LACE AND PAPER SHADE

Stitch the other end of the paper tube to the second ring. This paper base should now be covered with net. Cut a double circle of net for the top and pleat strips of net round the shade, stitching them neatly into place on the rings.

One-and-a-half-inch ribbon is used for the trimming. Make a ruching of the ribbon and stitch over the top seam, then gather the ribbon to a frill and stitch round the bottom of the frame. Make several small rosettes of the net and stitch them to the centre of the top of the shade, or one or two very tiny artificial flowers could be placed in the centre to finish the shade. However, do not use too much decoration, as the whole point of this type of shade is its daintiness. Many ideas will occur to the handicraft worker which can be carried out in this way, combining paper and fabric. For example, a lampshade to resemble a drum could very easily be made to use in a small boy's room.

CHAPTER VIII

Stiff lampshade covers: Paper shades — pleated lampshade — pie-frill lampshade covers — "Coolie Hat" type of cover — fluted shade in buckram — velvet and parchment shade.

BUCKRAM and paper are two very useful materials for covering lampshades, as they can be used either separately or combined with other materials which require stiffening. Both can be decorated by painting in various ways or by attaching motifs in felt or coloured paper to them. Paper lampshades are particularly useful where a long-lasting shade is not required. They are attractive in appearance, and being inexpensive may be changed frequently when soiled.

Paper lends itself easily to pleating and folding. Good-quality cartridge paper should be used for the covers, and before commencing a shade the pleating should be practised on some oddments of stiff paper, as once it is creased the paper cannot be uncreased. It is therefore necessary to be very sure where the pleats are to be formed before commencing a shade.

The first shade described is shown in Fig. 29A. It is a simple, straight pleated paper shade. This style is most suitable for large standard shades, but it may also be used to cover a pendant or table lamp. A pleated cover of this kind requires an "Empire" shape foundation frame which need not have side members, as the paper will be stiff enough to hold the rings in position. Commence by inspecting the wire rings and then binding them with bias tape, or painting the wires in a colour which will tone with the paper cover.

The width of the paper for the cover should be the depth of the frame plus about 2 in., to overhang the edges of the frame at top and bottom; the length of the paper should be three times the circumference of the ring at the bottom of the shade. The paper can be joined to obtain the necessary length, if the pieces are pleated first, then joined as shown in Fig. 29A. The pleats may be any size, but normally they are about 1 in. wide when used for an average-sized frame.

Lightly mark the position of each pleat on the edges of the paper with a pencil. The folding must be done with great care, and a piece of thin smooth wood a little longer than the width of the paper will be a great help in folding the pleats. Place the

64

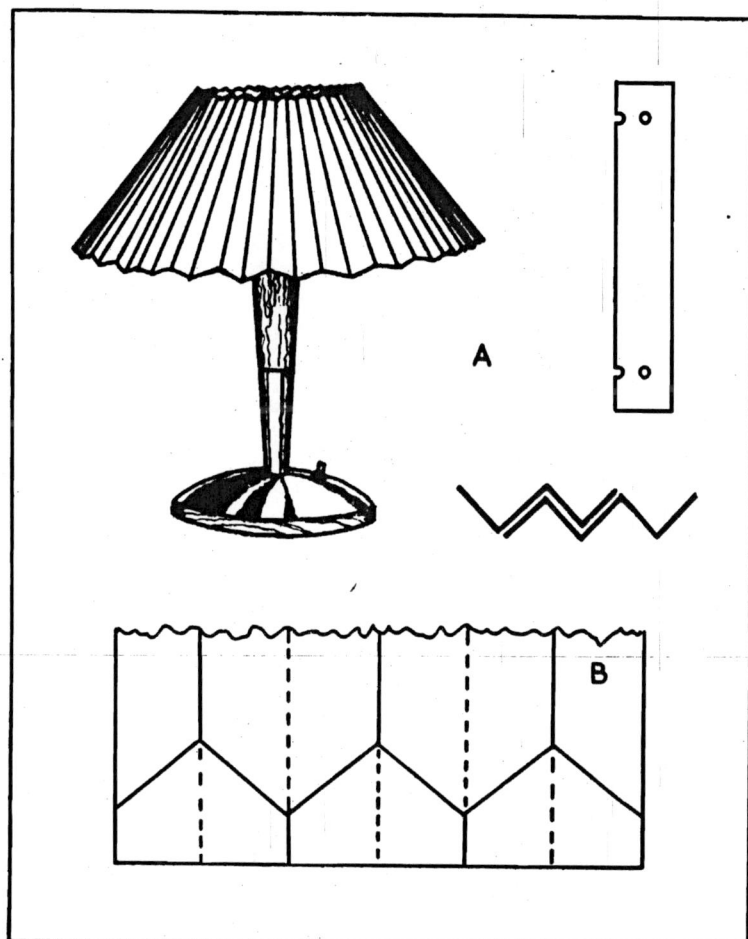

FIG. 29. PLEATING PAPER COVERS

length of paper on the edge of a flat surface and place the strip
of wood under the paper, with an edge level with the pencil marks,
and press the paper down to obtain a neat fold. The paper will
need to be worked backwards and forwards several times to make
a good fold.

After all the paper has been pleated, holes must be punched
through the centre of the pleats about 1 in. from either end, and
the holes should be large enough to allow a silk cord to be
threaded through them. Small nicks should next be cut in the

inside fold of the pleats, just below the punched holes—these nicks are required to hold the pleated cover to the rings of the frame. The cord should be inserted through the large holes. With this done, place the cover over the frame and draw the cords up tightly without crushing the paper; place the pleats evenly round the frame before tying the ends of the cords. The spacing of the holes and the nicks is shown in Fig. 29.

A very pretty variation of these pleated shades is obtained by using coloured "Cellophane" over cartridge paper. Make up a plain "Empire" shape cover in cartridge paper and stitch it to a wire frame, then pleat the "Cellophane" on to the paper shade, sticking each pleat top and bottom with transparent "Cellophane" tape. A narrow gimp or velvet ribbon can then be stitched over the tape to finish the cover.

Pie-frill lampshade covers in pleated paper have been introduced to this country from Scandinavia and have become very popular. The material required for a pie-frill shade should be about three times the required length of pleated cover, and the width should be the height of the frame plus an overlap of 2 in. or 3 in. top and bottom. The piece of paper for the cover should be lightly marked in pencil for 1-in. pleats, following the diagram in Fig. 29 for the markings. Mark the paper very lightly with pencil, so that the marks can later be removed with a soft rubber.

After marking the pleat lines the guide lines for the frills must be marked. In this shade the frill turns under at the top and the bottom of the cover, but many variations of this can be worked. Next the short crease lines should be marked from the guide lines (see Fig. 29B). It is most important to appreciate that some of the pleats fold outwards and some of them fold inwards. To clarify this, the diagram shows those that fold out by a continuous line, and those which fold in by a series of dashes.

With all the crease lines marked, the cover should be scored. Do this with a blunt tool guided by a straight-edge, and keep the pressure even. The next part of the work consists of folding, and this is best done on a smooth flat surface. If the scoring has been done properly the paper should fold easily without cracking. Fold each pleat and turning separately; it is not very easy to turn a well-shaped pleat at first, and some practice may be required. Do not crease all the pleats first and then the turnings, thinking to make things easier, or you may become confused with the "unders" and "overs." Work slowly and methodically until all the cover has been pleated. The ends will need to be overlapped and glued to hold them firmly.

The next step in the work is to mount the cover on the frame, and there are two ways in which this can be done. The cover may be stitched to the tape of the bound frame at the points where the turned-in folds touch the frame—if this course is adopted care must be taken to space the pleats evenly—or the cover may be joined to the frame by punching small holes through each inner fold, where it will meet the frame. Diagonal slits are then made from the holes to the edges, so that the frame wire can be slipped through these cuts to rest in the holes.

The simplest shape of all to make in paper is the "Coolie Hat" type of cover, and this style of frame is very popular in France, where they are often used three or four in a room, each one tinted a different colour. For this only one foundation ring is required, and this must include the gimbal fitting. For a pendant shade the point of the hat hangs downwards, while for a reading lamp it points upwards.

To make the "Coolie Hat" shade cover, cut a circle of paper with the diameter of the circle measuring about 2 in. to 3 in. larger than the diameter of the wire ring. Cut a line from the outer edge to the centre of the paper, then start stitching it to the wire ring, which should previously have been bound with bias binding. Continue stitching around the ring until the paper meets and cut away the surplus wedge of paper, allowing a margin for gumming the two edges together. It will be found that, as progress is made round the wire frame with the stitching, the shape will form itself. The depth of the cone can be altered; its size depends upon how much larger than the diameter of the wire ring the paper circle is cut.

A wide gimp should then be stitched over the join to the point of the "Coolie Hat" and back down the other side. Gimp should also be attached over the wire edge. If a hanging lamp is required, make the "coolie hat" shape with a plain wire ring without a gimbal, and attach cords to the edges by which it may be hung from the ceiling.

Buckram is one of the most useful materials for making lamp-shades, and is obtainable in white. It has an attractive appearance and can be tinted any shade quite easily by brushing over with water colour, though care must be taken not to make the material too damp, as this will make the buckram lose its stiffness; or it can be decorated by any of the painting methods; alternatively it can have designs, cut from other materials, stuck to it.

A very simple flared shade in buckram is illustrated in Fig. 30. To make this you will require two wire rings and some buckram. Bind the rings with bias binding as has been previously described, then cut a circle of buckram having a diameter twice that of the bottom ring, and cut a circle the same size as the smaller ring from the centre of the buckram. Bind round the edges of the buckram circle with bias binding and stitch the buckram to the top ring, using matching cotton. Pin the lower edge of the buck-

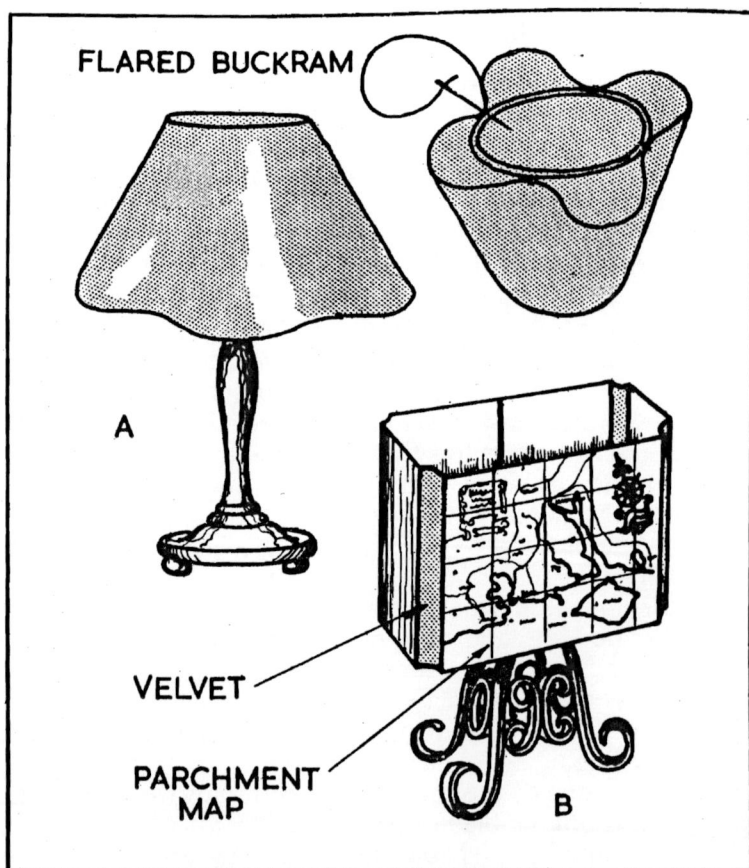

FIG. 30. FLARED SHADE

ram to the lower ring of the frame in wide flares, making sure the flares are all equally spaced, and stitch them to the frame where the buckram touches the ring. If a more decorative shade is required, stitch or gum the gimp round the edges of the frame.

It is often decided that a lampshade to match the curtains or covers in a room would be a good idea, and then the idea is dropped because of the difficulty of using the material as a lampshade covering. This is where buckram can be put to good use, especially when a very soft material is to be used as a cover. The buckram serves the dual purpose of a lining and a stiffening.

Inspect the foundation frame and bind it with bias binding. Next make a very accurate pattern and cut it out in the buckram. After cutting out the buckram, wipe over each piece with a damp sponge. There is no necessity to use a lot of water, use just enough to soften the glue in the buckram. Place the covering material over the buckram shapes, right side of the material facing you, and then place a damp cloth over it, then iron with a hot iron. The stiffening in the buckram softens and the material sticks to the buckram; for this reason it is necessary to use as hot an iron as the material will take without damaging it. It will be necessary to test the iron on some spare pieces before commencing, so as to obtain the right heat. When the material has been ironed on to the buckram leave it until it has cooled, then trim round the buckram shapes and make the cover in the usual way. When using patterned material for a panelled shade, make certain that the pattern runs the same way on all the panels, and if the pattern is large, that it is nicely centred on each pattern.

There is no necessity to cover all the shade with material; in some cases a pleasing effect can be obtained by cutting out the pattern motifs and sticking them on the buckram. Coloured laces or nets make very lovely shades if used over buckram in this way.

It is also possible to make many novelty shades by cutting out the shapes in buckram. A buckram shade can be decorated with gimp and fringe. In this case it is best to stick the decoration to the shade, using a white handicraft adhesive. Use only a small amount of the adhesive—if too much is used it will soak through the gimp and cause ugly stains. Buckram and velvet go together very well, and a plain buckram shade decorated with velvet bow, or with a velvet ribbon ruched around the edges, looks very effective. Buckram is easily tinted to any required colour. Use a large brush and brush over with water colour or fabric dye. Keep as dry as possible while working and leave to dry thoroughly before making up.

Velvet by itself, though a very lovely material, is not entirely suitable for lampshade making, as it is not sufficiently translucent to allow the light through, and secondly it has too "heavy" an appearance. However, velvet can be used to great advantage with other materials. The most usual combination is velvet and parchment. In describing this type of shade, real parchment is meant—not the imitation paper parchment, but parchment which is usually obtainable in the form of old maps, deeds, etc. The velvet is used only in small panels, to offset with its rich colour the creaminess of the parchment. This type of shade is suitable for dining rooms or lounges.

The shade illustrated in Fig. 30B is an oblong one and the four small corner panels are covered with velvet. This shape is very suitable for a reading lamp which is to stand on a table or against a wall.

These parchment maps and deeds, being very old, often require cleaning before being made into lampshades, and it is first necessary to find out if the writing on them is fast. To do this, test it in the following way. Wet a small part of the ink and cover the part with blotting paper; rub over the blotting paper with the unsharpened end of a pencil. Remove the blotting paper, and if it is unmarked the writing will withstand careful cleaning.

To clean the parchment mix a very weak solution of oxalic acid in water and wash the parchment with this. Use a sponge and work gently and quickly, and as soon as the parchment is clean, dry it with blotting paper. If the parchment deeds and maps are very old, and have creases and wrinkles in them, they will need a more thorough treatment to remove the fold creases; this treatment consists of re-backing the parchment, and is fully described in the book *Lampshade Making*[1] in the Foyles handbook series.

After cleaning and preparing the parchment, inspect and bind the frame. Then proceed to cover the narrow corner panels with velvet. Choose a rich dark colour—green or deep red are both good. Cut a strip of the material and place it over one of the corners. Pin the velvet to the binding at top and bottom edges of the frame, then pin the side of the strip of velvet to the side wires. Continue working in the manner described for fabric shades,

[1] *Lampshade Making*, by F. J. Christopher (Foyles, 2s. 6d.).

work round the corner piece, and, removing the pins one at a time, tighten the material and replace the pins. As these small panels are concave, the greatest stretch of the material must be down the length of the panel, so that the shape is maintained. Trim off any surplus material round the panel, leaving just enough to turn under. With a needle and suitably coloured thread stitch the panel to the binding on the wires. Fasten off securely and cover the other three corners in the same way.

Cut patterns for the two sides and two end panels in thin card, making quite certain that they are accurate. Position the panels on the parchment and mark and cut it to shape. The parchment is stitched to the frame, and as these old maps, etc., are often rather brittle, it is best to pierce stitch holes first, using a fine bradawl. Care must be taken not to break the material at the edges. Use a medium-sized needle and strong cotton and sew firmly, but on no account pull the cotton too tightly or it may cut the parchment. It is a great help to use clothes pegs or paper clips to hold the panel in position when stitching it.

For decorating the edges choose a simple gimp or braid to match the velvet, remembering that the velvet and old parchment have great beauty in themselves, and the purpose of the gimp is not really to "decorate" the shade but to neaten the edges and to complement the mellowed colouring of the parchment. If a fringe is required, choose one of the antique styles with a bobble edge rather than the straight rayon ones, which are more suitable for use with plastic materials.

CHAPTER IX

Basketry lampshades: Lampshade for a reading lamp — materials — method of weaving the shade — constructing the base — finishing — wiring the lampholder.

DURING the past few years woven basketry furniture has again become popular, and the idea of using basketry materials has now spread to lampshade making. It is little wonder that these basketry lampshades have become so popular. They are inexpensive to make, and look right in any but the most conventionally furnished rooms; also, these shades are practically indestructible, and can even be scrubbed with soap and water over and over again.

In Fig. 31 is illustrated a woven lampshade on a reading lamp the base of which is also basketry, and which is woven over an empty jar. Any kitchen will provide suitable jars for base foundations; empty pickle or honey jars are best, but any reasonably heavy bottle or jar will do.

Most basketry lampshades are made after the "Empire" shape, but it is possible to introduce considerable variety by means of various styles in edgings, by trimming in coloured raffia, or by introducing coloured wooden beads into the borders.

To make the shade shown in the illustration you will require a small wire ring containing a gimbal, a quantity of No. 3 cane for weaving (a pound by weight should be more than ample) and enough No. 6 cane to cut twenty-seven stakes 18 in. in length. The shade is worked on a cardboard base in the same way as one works cane on a wooden base, and when the shade is completed the cardboard is torn away.

To commence the basketry lampshade, cut out a circle of cardboard a little larger than the wire ring; place the wire ring on the cardboard circle and pencil round the outline of the wire. On this pencil line punch twenty-seven holes at equal distances apart, large enough to take the No. 6 cane. Soak the cane in water. Insert the 18-in. stakes into the holes and pull them through until they are about 4 in. above the cardboard. Tie the ends together on top of the cardboard, to keep them in position while the cover is being woven.

Soak the No. 3 cane in water to make it pliable, and work

72

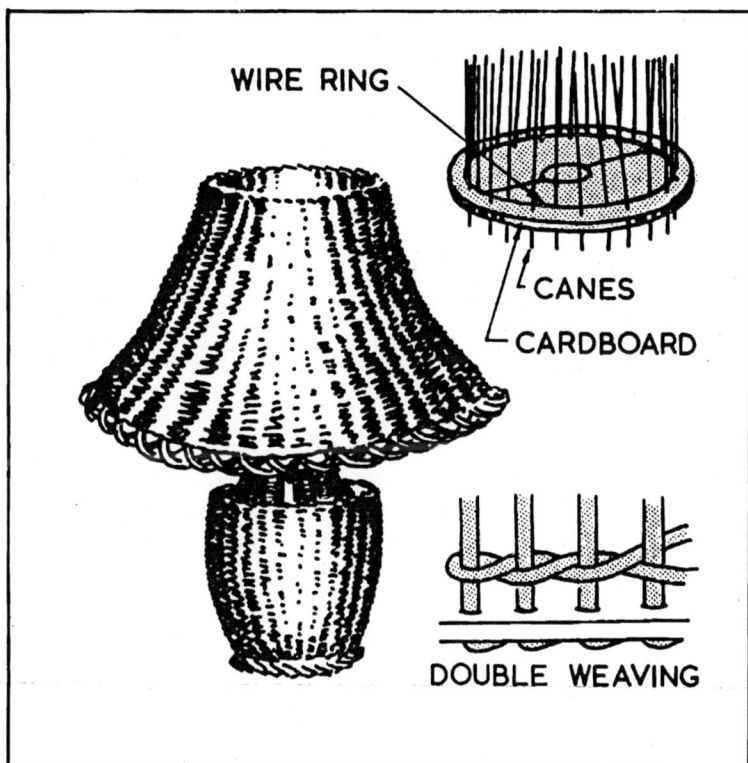

WIRE RING

CANES

CARDBOARD

DOUBLE WEAVING

FIG. 31. BASKETRY SHADE AND BASE

about 2 in. of basketry in single weaving, then proceed in double weaving, shaping the shade outwards all the time. Directions for working the single and double weaving can only be given briefly here, and the worker who intends to make any quantity of these shades is advised to study *Basketry*,[1] a companion volume in the Foyles handbook series.

Single weaving consists of taking the weaving cane in front of one stake and behind the next stake, all round the base, while double weaving consists of bending the weaving cane in two, crossing the two ends, and slipping the loop thus formed over the first stake, continuing to weave as shown in Fig. 31. Continue in double weaving, keeping the stakes bent outwards in a graceful

[1] *Basketry*, by F. J. Christopher (Foyles, 2s. 6d.).

curve until the shade is about 6 in. to 7 in. deep. Before commencing the border, soak the stakes for about fifteen minutes in
hot water so that they bend easily. Proceed by bending each stake
down behind one, in front of two, behind one, in front of two,
behind one, thus leaving the ends of the stakes inside the work.
The worker with a knowledge of basketry can work many fancy
openwork edges in place of this simple one.

Untie the bottom stakes and work the top of the shade. Place
the wire ring on the cardboard, with alternate stakes inside and
outside the ring; this is shown in the illustration Fig. 31. Work
the border in the same way as the bottom edge. Bend down a
stake and pass it behind two, in front of one, and behind the
next one, all the way round, so that the ends are inside the shade.
Leave until the stakes are quite dry again, then clip off the ends
near to the basket work, and tear away the cardboard to complete the shade. Should the basketry lampshade seem out of shape
when it is finished, it can be improved by soaking in hot water
for a few minutes and then bending to a better shape.

The base of the lamp illustrated is made from a stone 4-lb. jam
jar. A metal batten holder was purchased and bolted to the metal
lid of the one shown, to hold the bulb and flex. To make the
basketry cover for the jar, first wash and thoroughly dry the jar,
then make a base to fit the bottom of the jar. This may either be
cut out in plywood or in thick cardboard. Several thicknesses of
card can be glued together until the right thickness is obtained.
Make the base about ¼ in. larger all round than the base of the
bottle, punch an uneven number of holes round the base ¼ in. in
from the edge, and cut a stake of No. 6 cane for each hole about
6 in. longer than the height of the jar. Soak the cane and push
each stake through the holes until about 3 in. protrudes. Tie the
long ends of the stakes together, dampen the short ends, and
work them to make a border under the base as follows. Bend
down a stake, pass it behind two stakes, in front of the next stake,
and behind the next stake; repeat this all round the base so that
the points of the stakes are inside the work. Later, when the cane
has dried, the ends can be trimmed off close to the edge of the
work.

Untie the top stakes, and using soaked No. 5 cane and single
weaving, work one or two rounds over and under the stakes.
Place the jar or bottle inside the stakes. Continue weaving,
keeping the basketry pulled tightly to the sides of the jar, so that

it takes the exact shape of the jar. When the top is reached, finish with the same border as the base—that is, bend one stake behind two stakes, in front of one stake, behind one stake, only this time finish so that the ends are on the outside and the basketry is pulled tightly to the top of the lampstand. Leave till the canes have dried completely, then clip off the ends. The lampholder should be wired in the usual way and the flex may be tucked away inside the basketry cover of the base.

CHAPTER X

Table lamp bases: Converting bottles and jars — fitting a lamp
socket and switch — "Pifco" adaptor — use of a back-plate —
drilling a hole for the flex — suitable drills — precautions.

MANY of the lampshades described in this book are suitable for
use as covers for table lamps, and in addition to making attractive
lampshades, the home handicraft worker can make many very
effective bases for table lamps. A wide variety of ordinary articles
can quite simply be transformed into table lamps, and some
suggestions are given in Fig. 32.

Bottles and jars are favourites for conversion to table-lamp

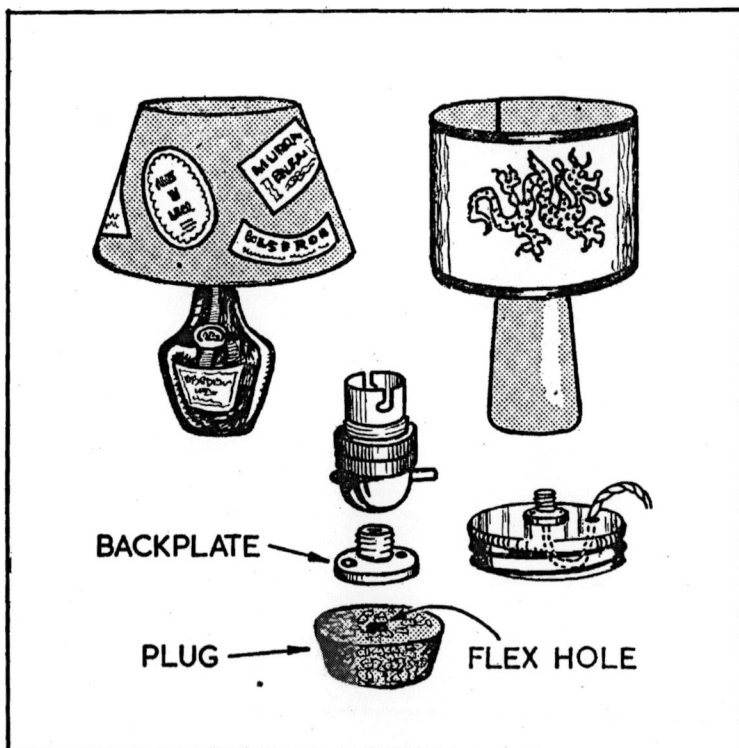

BACKPLATE

PLUG

FLEX HOLE

FIG. 32.   TABLE-LAMPS

bases, and other articles that may be used for this purpose include vases, candlesticks, large polished pieces of wood, and various kinds of ornaments. In most cases converting any article to a lamp base consists in fitting the object with a lamp socket and switch so that it may easily and efficiently be wired for electric current.

Converting jars and bottles, vases and ornaments with lids or necks is a fairly simple matter. This can be done by using a special adaptor made for this purpose. This is the "Pifco" adaptor, which consists of a socket to take the electric bulb and switch together as one unit, that is secured to a cork. The cork is fashioned as a roll which may be adjusted to fit most bottles with no neck. If this type of fitting is used for converting a bottle into a lampshade base, it will be necessary to make provision for fitting the flex which is attached to the lampholder through a central hole in the cork stopper. For this it will be necessary to drill a hole in the glass, and this is described later in this chapter.

Wine bottles make very attractive lamp bases, and the design motif may be emphasized by attaching labels from wine bottles to the shade, if it has a smooth cover. Parchment lends itself extremely well to this type of cover, and the labels and cover . should be given a coat of clear varnish so that they may easily be cleaned without damage.

A method of fitting wide-necked jars and bottles with a lampholder socket is by using what is known as a back-plate. This is illustrated in Fig. 32. The back-plate may be soldered or bolted to a metal jar cover or closure of wood or cork that has been cut to shape to fit the top of a bottle or jar. The back-plate may be screwed into the main material. If a back-plate is used the lamp socket must be of the type which is fitted with an internal thread which screws over the threaded base of the back-plate. In the case of a wide-necked jar or bottle the flex hole may be made in a closure as illustrated in Fig. 32, and the socket may be of the type fitted with a switch, or a separate "torpedo" switch may be fitted to the flex. For this type of lamp base a batten-holder type of lamp socket may be successfully used in place of the back-plate and holder.

The batten holder is attached to the closure of the jar, which may be cork, wood, or a metal lid, by bolting or screwing it in place, and if a batten holder is used it will also be necessary to make provision for the entry of the flex, so that it may be attached to the connections of the lampholder.

If the flex is to run through the lamp base it will be necessary to make a hole for this purpose. If the base is wood it will be found a simple matter to drill a hole for the flex, but if the table-lamp base is of glass, stoneware or china, it will not be quite so easy to make the necessary hole. In most towns this can be done locally by taking the base with the position of the hole marked to a hardware merchant or builders' merchant, who will very often drill glass and china at the owner's risk.

The drilling may also be done by the lampshade maker, and for this purpose special drill bits may be obtained. These may be used with the electrically powered drills or with hand drills. These special drills with hardened points are normally used for drilling holes in brick, stone, tile, marble, cement or slate, and although they are not specially manufactured for drilling glass or china-ware, they may be successfully used provided reasonable care is taken while the work is being done. In this work it is essential to ensure that a firm and even pressure is maintained while the drill is being rotated against the material.

It will be found necessary to mark the point of entry in the material to be drilled, and this can be done with the tang of a file. It is necessary to make only a very small indentation, so that the point of the drill is guided and does not "wander" as the drill is rotated.

Full details of the use of carbon-tipped drills, which are manufactured under various trade names, may be obtained from the suppliers, and the drills are available in a very large range of sizes. For the flex of most types of lamp a $\frac{1}{4}$-in. drill will be found a suitable size.

During the drilling of glass or chinaware it is advisable to use a lubricant to prevent the tool and material from becoming over-heated. A suitable lubricant for this purpose can be made by dissolving crushed camphor in turpentine. During the work of drilling it is important to ensure that the drill is pressed firmly into the hole being cut as the drill is rotated, and the direction of the drill should not be changed. If this is done the glass or china-ware will in all probability crack or split.

Care must be taken in wiring the lamp base to ensure that the connections are properly made. The covering of the flex should not be frayed, and connections both to the adaptor and the plug should be made so that the ends of the wire are securely held and sufficient insulation is provided to prevent the two wires of the flex from touching. If the worker has no knowledge at all of electrical wiring it is advised that this be done by a competent electrician.

CHAPTER XI

Decorating lampshades: Tinting — painted designs — transfers — coloured paper shapes — floral motifs — repeating design — wax crayon designs — fringes and braids — lace decoration — "shadow" work — gathered or pleated frills — ruching — shell edging — Toby frills — knitted fringe.

A WELL-MADE lampshade does not require much in the way of decoration, as most of the materials used have their own beauty. However, many lampshades may require some embellishment, used discreetly. Much depends upon the purpose of the shade and the general furnishing and colour scheme of the room in which the shade is used.

Parchment, vellum and stiff paper shades are often improved by tinting the inside of the covers with a warm soft pink or yellow, and, being very plain in themselves, these materials make a perfect background for many forms of decoration. As a rule these shades do not appear at their best sporting large velvet bows or fabric ruchings, but they do look good with a painted design or decorative stuck-on labels, or even a carefully executed design built up of coloured paper shapes. Alternatively, a wide variety of coloured transfers can be purchased, and these are ideal for use on parchment.

Decorating can be carried out before the shade is made up, but in some cases it will be found easier to do the decorating after making the shade, and, unless you are an artist, you will find it necessary to trace the design on to the parchment or paper before making up the shade.

Designs may be traced very easily on to parchment or vellum, because of its translucency. Draw or trace the design on a piece of white paper (do not use a ball-point pen for this, as the ink may rub off) and place the drawn design under the vellum. Then lightly pencil in the outlines of the design, which will clearly be seen through the parchment. Fig. 33 shows several decorative designs which are made up from the type of transfers easily obtained from handicraft dealers or stationers.

In all branches of handicrafts there are craftworkers who spoil a well-made and finely designed piece of work by either over-decoration or insufficient finishing. A good finish is very necessary to lampshade making, and as this is one of the crafts in which you

FIG. 33. TRANSFERS

can "see it growing" the finishing processes should not be unduly hurried. The good craftsman does not try to hide inferior work with decoration. Braids and fringes will not hide blemishes or inadequately finished lampshades.

It is not necessary to be an artist to be able to put a satisfactory finishing touch to a lampshade. It is largely a matter of using suitable materials and practice in applying the various types of decoration, although it is also largely a matter of personal taste. Obviously it is only common sense for the worker who wishes to sell the goods produced to bear in mind the modern trend of simplicity in line and form and the avoidance of over-decoration.

Quick and attractive décor results can be obtained by using coloured paper shapes on parchment or vellum lampshades. These very colourful shapes may be purchased in boxes of assorted shapes for a few pence and, being ready gummed, take only a few moments to put into place. They can be made up into an endless variety of amusing and attractive "repeat" designs. If the worker has plenty of time to put into the project, there is great scope in making wall friezes to match the lampshades. Many suitable motifs may be devised for decorating the walls and lampshades for shops, nurseries, kitchens and bathrooms.

Some suitable designs are shown in Fig. 33. It should of course be the craftworker's aim to produce original designs, but those without any great artistic ability will find a wealth of ideas in embroidery transfers. Often it is possible to combine parts of two or three transfers to produce a really interesting design.

Small circles about the size of a sixpence may be used to great advantage. For instance, a plain "Empire" style frame can be covered with a creamy-coloured parchment, with the top and bottom of the shade bound with a deep blue *passe partout*, then blue circles of paper can be stuck at intervals all over the shade; or a pale rose-coloured sheepskin parchment with silver trimmings may be worked. There are endless variations of colour schemes for this treatment. Another idea can be worked by attaching small circles of paper in many colours, overlapping each other all round the top and bottom of a shade.

On panelled shades, floral motifs make lovely corner decorations, but care must be taken not to over-elaborate the decorating of lampshades, and it is not necessary to place a motif in every panel. Floral designs are easy to work and have the advantage of fitting into almost any colour scheme. A spray of flowers will introduce ample colour if the lampshade covering is plain— motifs made up from bell-shaped flowers, sprays of blossom or autumn leaves are all very attractive and colourful. When making these motifs there is no need to cut each piece separately to shape; the various shapes may be selected from the boxes of mixed paper shapes obtainable or, if preferred, they may be cut from strips of gummed paper. The design must be worked out in colour, then the various parts traced on to thin card, and the card cut out and used as a pattern. Several thicknesses of gummed paper can be cut at the same time with sharp scissors.

If a repeating design is being used, a strip of paper can be bent as shown in Fig. 34. After folding, the motif design should be traced on to the paper and all the folds cut through together. Remember that parts of the side lines of the paper must not be cut to result in a long shaped strip. Choose a simple pattern for

POINTS TO
TOUCH
UNCUT
SIDES

FIG. 34. REPEATING DECORATIVE DESIGNS

the first attempt, and practise on some strips of newspaper first.

If any difficulty is experienced in making the paper shapes stick to the parchment, wipe over the area to be decorated with "Thawpit," which will remove the grease from the parchment. To finish, when all the design is stuck on, coat the shade with clear varnish.

There are two main ways in which a fabric-covered shade may be decorated. The fabric itself may be decorated, or trimmings may be added by using gimps, braids, fringes, etc. In most cases it will be found best to paint or dye the fabric before making up the cover.

Perhaps the simplest way of doing this is with children's ordinary wax crayons. When fixed, these colours are quite fast to light, and if necessary may be washed and ironed. This method is a very inexpensive way of producing the most luxurious-looking hand-coloured shades. For a few pence one can buy a packet of these crayons. Almost any smooth material which can be ironed with a fairly warm iron is suitable for this type of decoration, but washing satin is widely used for lampshade covering and is particularly good.

In most cases it will be necessary to decorate the material before covering the shade. Have ready an iron and a table or other flat surface on which you can iron. Decide on a suitable design—a small motif as shown in Fig. 34 can be scattered all over the material and makes a good design for practising, but if you feel that free-hand drawing is beyond you, embroidery transfers are very useful for obtaining design shapes. If the material is transparent, slip the design underneath the material and colour on the top of it. If using embroidery transfers, try to choose a yellow one, so that the outlines will not mark the material too much.

Having transferred the design outlines on the material, the next stage is to commence the colouring with the crayons. Place a large sheet of blotting paper on the table. Pin the material on top of the blotting paper, with the right side of the material uppermost. The blotting paper should have previously been heated by ironing it, and the iron should be kept hot while the work is in progress, so that the blotting paper can be re-ironed at intervals to keep it warm. A little practice will soon indicate how hot the paper should be. If it is too cool, it will not draw the crayon colours through the material, but if it is too hot it will melt the crayon too quickly and the colours will run. One colour may be used on top of another for shading—in fact, the colouring is done exactly as if the picture were being crayoned on paper. When all the colouring has been done, it is necessary to fix the colour—and this is done by placing a piece of blotting paper on top and beneath the work, and ironing over the top of the pile.

It is possible to buy a great variety of fringes and braids for decorating lampshades, but some of them are rather expensive. The craftworker will often find that a more attractive finish can be obtained by making one's own frills and ruches, especially for the more luxurious type of shade.

A peach silk shade of simple shape for a bedroom may be improved by two or three rows of black or coffee-coloured lace round top and bottom, as shown in Fig. 35. First pull the drawing thread which is woven in the straight edge of the net or lace to gather it, and attach the frill either by stitching with whipping stitch or sticking it to the cover with one of the white handicraft adhesives. Small lace motifs attached to a silk shade give it a very pleasing effect when the lamp is lit. A white buckram shade can be completely covered with black or coloured lace, and this is easily done. The cover should be cut out in buckram and covered with a piece of lace, and ironed with a fairly hot iron over a damp cloth—this will cause the stiffening in the buckram to soften and hold the lace in place. Leave the cover for a short time to allow the stiffening to harden, then make up the shade in the usual way.

Another very attractive method of decorating a plain buckram shade is by "shadow" work. To do this a piece of georgette or other sheer material to cover the buckram is required, also some scraps of material in a deeper shade and some embroidery silk. First mark out a small, simple floral design on the georgette, and work the leaves and stems very neatly in back-stitch so that there are no visible joins or knots. Cut the small pieces of material to roughly the shapes of the flowers and place them between the buckram and georgette, so that they show through under the flowers in the design. Iron the buckram and georgette, protecting the materials with a damp cloth, then make up the shade in the usual way. When lit the effect will be of shadowy flowers showing through the cover.

Simple gathered frills or pleated frills and various types of ruching all make most decorative edges for fabric-covered lampshades. Fig. 35 shows five types of inexpensive edgings which can be really glamorous. Fig. 35A is a straight gathered frill of the same material as the shade itself. For this style cut a straight strip of material about ½ in. wider than the finished frill is to be, and approximately one and a half times to twice the required length. Neaten one long edge with a narrow hem, the other long edge is turned over about ¼ in. and pressed. Run a gathering thread through this edge, dip the frill in a solution of plastic starch, dry and iron it, then pull the gathering thread until the

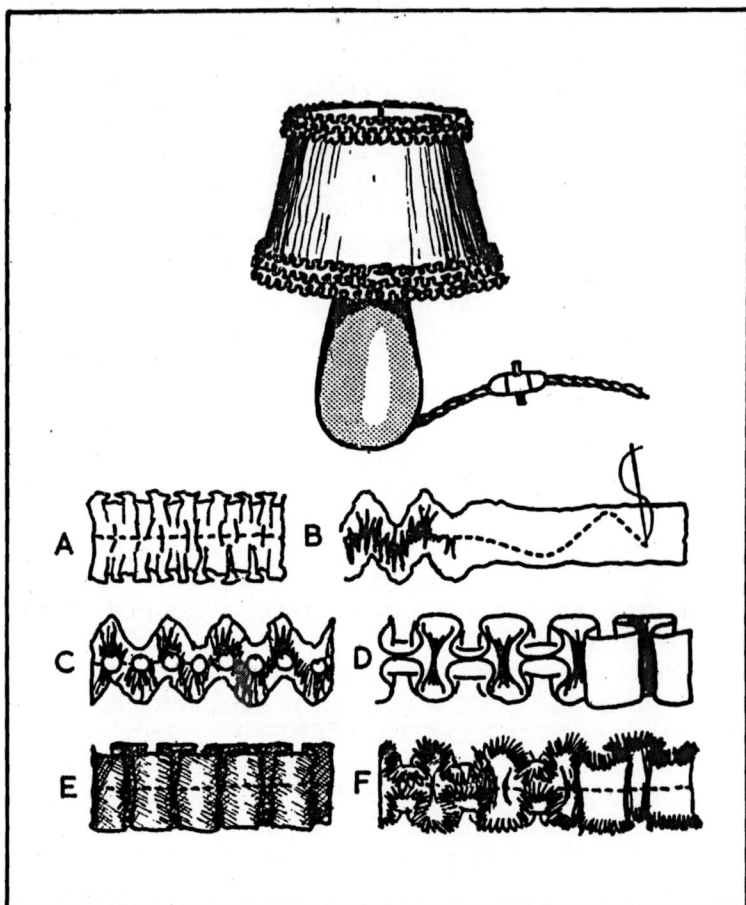

FIG. 35. EDGINGS

frill is the required length, then lightly stitch to edge of frame with matching thread.

Fig. 35B shows a shell gathering which makes an attractive edge. For this a length of material about 2 in. wide is required, or if ribbon is used it should be about 1 in. wide and at least twice as long as the finished length is to be.

If strips of the lampshade covering material are being used, turn both edges of each strip over on the wrong side and press well. Run a gathering thread along the folded material or ribbon, working the stitching zigzag up to the top edge and down to the bottom edge. Repeat the zigzag stitching keeping the points about 1 in. apart on each edge, and draw the gathering thread up until the zigzags form a straight line. This trimming may be lightly stitched to the edges of the shade, or it may be cemented to the cover with a colourless adhesive such as "Mystic." When using frills and ruchings as trimmings avoid handling them as much as possible, so that they keep their fresh, crisp appearance.

The finish in Fig. 35c is similar to shell edging, and it may be made in a contrasting material or with strips of the covering material. For a rather special trimming use gold or silver thread for the stitching and stitch a tiny pearl between each shell.

Commence by cutting strips, about 1½ in. wide, on the cross of the material. Fold each over on the wrong side of the material and seam. Turn the tubes thus made the right side out with the help of a safety pin, as shown in the illustration. Press well so that the roll of material lies flat and smooth. Thread a longish needle with a double thread of sewing silk or stranded cotton, and pierce the strips to bring out the needle on the right side of the material (see the diagram). Put the needle vertically behind the roll and not through it, with the thread held under the needle, pull the needle through upwards and towards the worker and draw the thread very tight. Pass the needle along the inside of the roll, putting it in on the right side of the knot just made, and bring it out again about ¼ in. to ½ in. away, depending upon the width of the roll.

In Fig. 35d is illustrated a very effective Toby frill. For use on lampshades this type of edging is usually made in velvet or taffeta ribbon. If other material is used, choose a very stiff one such as starched muslin or organdie. The strips for this type of frill are cut on the straight of the material and the strips of material are pinned into box pleats along each edge, then machined or backstitched with matching thread through the middle of the pleats. To make a Toby frill, three times the length of the finished frill in material or ribbon is required. Lightly catch the top and bottom of each pleat together as shown in the illustration.

Net makes a very pretty frill, requiring two to three times the finished length of the edge being treated. Cut strips of net and gather or pleat them, then stitch along their centre. The frill illustrated in Fig. 35e shows the net box-pleated.

A slightly more elaborate type of ruching is the rose ruching shown in Fig. 35F. This is made by cutting strips of taffeta on the bias about 1½ in. wide. The edges of the strips are then frayed to a depth of about 3/16 in. on each edge. Box-pleat the strips, pinning the pleats at top and bottom, and with matching thread stitch through the centre of the strip, picking up the centre of each pleat and joining it to its neighbour, so that a circular rose is formed, as in the illustration.

Such a wide variety of fringes can be purchased at reasonable cost that it is not always necessary to make them, but when making a special shade you may be unable to obtain a fringe of just the right shade of colour. In these cases it is very simple to knit a fringe, which may be worked in either single or double cotton. Number 12 knitting needles are used and a strip of very thick card the depth of the required fringe is also required.

Begin by casting on seven stitches with the cotton, then proceed as follows:

First Row.—Insert the needle in the first stitch in the usual way, take the strip of card and hold it between the thumb and first finger of the left hand close up to the work. Pass the thread along the back and then up the front of the mesh, and round the point of the right-hand needle. Knit off the stitch, keeping it close to the card on which the fringe is wound. Knit the following stitch plain, then make one stitch, knit two together, make one, knit two together, knit one.

Next Row.—Slip the first stitch and knit six. Repeat these two rows alternately for the length required. When the card is covered with loops, those at one end can be slipped off to make room for more. A twist is given to the loops of the fringe by inserting a knitting needle in the loop and twisting tightly, then drawing the needle out.

Lampshade making is a craft of unlimited scope, and is one that can bring much pleasure by profitably occupying spare time. Many more ideas for novel and practical shades not mentioned in this book because of lack of space will occur to the lampshade maker, who with a little experience will be able to adapt them to his needs. There is a good market for the completed lampshades, provided they are well made and reasonably priced.

Lightning Source UK Ltd.
Milton Keynes UK
UKOW03f2356030614

232810UK00001B/68/P